# THE BEST PARTY OF OUR LIVES

## STORIES of GAY WEDDINGS
### and True Love to Inspire Us All

Sarah Galvin

SASQUATCH BO[

SEATTLE

D0061716

Printed in the United States of America

Published by Sasquatch Books
19 18 17 16 15          9 8 7 6 5 4 3 2 1

Editor: Hannah Elnan
Production editor: Emma Reh
Design: Anna Goldstein
Cover photograph: Charity Burggraaf
Copyeditor: Janice Lee

Lines from "Mouthful of Forevers" reprinted with permission
from Andrews McMeel Publishing

Library of Congress Cataloging-in-Publication Data is available.

ISBN: 978-1-63217-013-2

Sasquatch Books
1904 Third Avenue, Suite 710
Seattle, WA 98101
(206) 467-4300
www.sasquatchbooks.com
custserv@sasquatchbooks.com

Certified Chain of Custody
SUSTAINABLE  Promoting Sustainable Forestry
FORESTRY
INITIATIVE  www.sfiprogram.org
SFI-01268

SFI label applies to the text stock

PRAISE FOR *The Best Party of Our Lives*

"We've reached a watershed moment in the history of marriage, and Galvin marks it in the most profound way possible: by telling the human stories of those most deeply affected. As universal as it is personal, this is a book to be treasured by anyone who believes in the power of love."

**—ELLEN MCCARTHY, author of *The Real Thing: Lessons on Love and Life from a Wedding Reporter's Notebook***

"*The Best Party of Our Lives* is as informational (did you know that the International Association of Gay Square Dance Clubs is a thing?) as it is moving as it is laugh out loud funny. On the heels of marriage equality nationwide, this book shows us that the party is just getting started."

**—ZACH WAHLS, *New York Times* best-selling author of *My Two Moms: Lessons of Love, Strength, and What Makes a Family***

"Prepare for your heart to beat faster, your smile to spread wider, and your confidence in the power of love to soar. In these true stories of true love, Sarah Galvin proves that all love is equal—and equally moving—by distilling the essence of the bonds that tie us together as members of the human family, whether gay, lesbian, trans, or otherwise. Grab this book, uncork the champagne, and let the celebrations begin!"

**—ANN BAUSUM, award-winning author of social justice history including *Stonewall: Breaking Out in the Fight for Gay Rights***

"Twenty-three weddings lead to twenty-three stories about love, life, and even loss. Woven through these narratives are Sarah Galvin's rapier wit and observations that bring each celebration alive on the page. Reading this book will make you want to invite Sarah Galvin to your wedding."

**—JASON SCHMIDT, author of *A List of Things That Didn't Kill Me***

ALSO BY SARAH GALVIN

*The Three Einsteins*

# CONTENTS

## PART IV: RECEPTION

## PART V: THE HAPPILY EVER AFTER PARTY

# INTRODUCTION

BECAUSE I'VE ALWAYS FIGURED I'D MOST likely spend my life with a woman, getting married was something I'd never really thought about before same-sex marriage was legalized in Washington. Honestly, the legal situation barely mattered, though, because marriage didn't seem that relevant to my life. My parents divorced when I was twelve, and the only significant ceremonial family gathering I can recall after that involved four people scattering my grandpa's ashes under a bust of Freud. I had family members who were married, but the big topic of discussion in the family was usually the arts. There was plenty of conversation about love, but any kind of love was considered desirable—nobody really mentioned marriage.

I certainly had no interest in weddings—I had the impression that they involved a boring time in a church followed by a bad dance party and, best-case scenario, free drinks. In 2012, though, I got a summer job at a catering company that owned two wedding venues, and over the course of one season, the number of weddings I'd attended jumped from maybe two to over fifty. Sometimes the venue booked two weddings a day. It was surreal and a little disconcerting to lay out one couple's polished rocks and bags of monogrammed candies and then make way for the next couple's color-coordinated napkins and shot glasses. I served enough champagne to fill a Cadillac and enough hors d'oeuvres to bury one. I saw couples who seemed meant to be together and ones I'd give about two months. I had no dreams of my own wedding yet, but whether maneuvering trays of hors d'oeuvres around bouquets of red roses or blow-up dolls dressed as cowboys, I noticed how each wedding reflected the relationship it celebrated. It was fascinating and often beautiful.

In this venue there were, as tradition dictated, separate rooms where the grooms and best men and the brides and bridesmaids convened before the ceremony, and I always felt a little uncomfortable bussing or bringing drinks there. The room for women was all pink and tulle, and the room for the men resembled a ski lodge. There was a wall in the grooms' room where decades of newlywed men had pinned their boutonnieres, and as someone who's refused to wear a dress since the age of five, I absolutely knew that should I get married, my boutonniere belonged among them, at least in spirit. But of course, I wasn't welcome in that room, under those circumstances. It was the first time I can recall feeling personally excluded by laws against same-sex marriage. Several other queer people worked there, and I remember one of them quit. It had bothered him too much.

The following year, I began writing a column called Wedding Crasher, a series of write-ups of local weddings, for the *Stranger*, Seattle's alt-weekly newspaper. (No actual crashing was involved—the paper received a handful of invitations a month.) The column began in celebration of the overturning of the Defense of Marriage Act (DOMA) in the *Windsor v. United States* trial. Soon after DOMA (which dictated that no state was obligated to recognize the legal validity of a same-sex relationship even if it was recognized as marriage by another state, and defined marriage for the purposes of federal law as the union of a man and woman) was found to be unconstitutional, same-sex marriage was legalized in Washington.

For years, the *Stranger* had run a Party Crasher column, which I adored. There was an open invitation to request a *Stranger* writer's presence at any Seattle-area party, and every week staff would pick out the most appealing and send someone to cover it. I started reading Party Crasher as a teenager, before I was old enough to go to real parties, and it was my favorite column in the paper. Every week I flung open the newspaper box on the corner by my high school, full of anticipation. My reaction to the glimpse of adult freedom Party Crasher provided was something like an aspiring pioneer's first visions of the frontier.

It was hard to believe some of the scenarios in Party Crasher existed outside of movies—there were, for instance, a party celebrating the addition of a stripper pole to a privately owned hearse and a party involving several marching bands and a game of tetherball where the ball was on fire. I soon began hosting my own parties at every opportunity (i.e., whenever my mom was out of town). The most memorable of these was "Trashmas," which happened in spring and involved a large quantity of garbage, Livingston screw-top wine, and old Christmas decorations my friends collected from neighbors' driveways. Also of note: a party hosted in a garage-sized house my friends and I built out of cardboard and gay porn, where our all-girl GG Allin cover band played its first show. The latter, especially, made me realize that with enough work (and duct tape and slightly damp cardboard), it is possible to manifest dreams into reality.

The parties my friends and I threw as kids were strange and grand because they aspired to be something none of us really knew or understood yet. I'm happy to say experience hasn't destroyed the allure (though I won't be stocking a party with Livingston again anytime soon). What most interests me about parties is their ability to suspend reality, their potential as a venue for a sort of collective self-expression, and the challenge of anticipating a group's desires and creating an environment in which those desires are satisfied to an unprecedented extent.

I wanted to do the same thing with writing. I began freelancing for the *Stranger* when I was twenty-four, and of course, one of my first requests was to become the new author of Party Crasher, which hadn't run in a year or two. The *Stranger*'s politics had always appealed to me as much as its evocative accounts of strip shows in hearses, and when the editors described the wedding column they wanted me to write, I wished I could call my fifteen-year-old self and tell me what the future held.

Wedding Crasher offered coverage of any wedding, but because of its intentionally celebratory timing following the approval of Referendum 74 (which made same-sex marriage legal in Washington) and the *Stranger*'s history of gay rights advocacy, more than half of the weddings I attended were same-sex—the first gay weddings I'd ever seen. At these weddings I was struck for the first time by the odd nature of gay history, which unlike most other types of cultural history is not inherited. Though I wasn't related to anyone at these weddings, I felt I was participating in a special kind of family gathering I had never attended before. I often sensed an unspoken understanding between myself, the marrying couples, and other queer guests that we were celebrating a shared victory.

I was blown away by things I saw. Even more so than my catering job, Wedding Crasher proved that weddings were not what I had previously assumed. I went to a black-metal wedding where a banner that read "For the greater glory of Satan" in Latin hung over the altar, a brunch wedding attended by members of the Portland Masturbation Club, and a wedding that was mostly a Wild Turkey–fueled dance party in a driveway.

I expected I would have fun at strangers' weddings, but I was surprised by how emotional they made me—I think I cried at every one. I became friends with many of the newlyweds, and they were my first interview subjects for this book.

Weddings entail all of the most appealing features of the best kinds of parties, with one added element—they are celebrations of one of the greatest events of human life. Love, like death, is something that's impossible to honor adequately. It would take another entire lifetime to celebrate the life of someone whose life has ended, and it would take a party of love's magnitude to properly celebrate that love. Celebration on this scale is impossible, yet people feel a deep need for it. I would venture to guess both art and religion began as responses to this need.

I suppose I didn't expect to become emotional at strangers' weddings because I hadn't witnessed the development of their relationships and had no personal attachment to them. I liked many of these people immediately, but that wasn't why I cried when they exchanged vows or shared their first kiss in front of everyone important to them. It was the intersection of the personal and the universal that affected me.

Humans have the capacity to be aware of things beyond their comprehension—like the dimensions of the sun or the desire to see another person every day for a lifetime, even though they have awful taste in shoes and their snore sounds like a slide whistle. Though I wasn't familiar with these people or their relationships, I recognized in the representation of love's minutiae at their weddings a celebration of something beyond comprehension that resonated deeply with me. Perhaps because of weddings in popular media, in the past I'd thought of a wedding as a ritual that was the same for everyone, like getting a driver's license renewed. To see the variety of ways people express their love—including queer people and poor people like me—made weddings seem personally relevant and even, dare I say, desirable.

I took a break from Wedding Crasher when I got into the University of Washington's poetry MFA program. That experience, which I would compare (mostly positively) to being shot out of a cannon, was nearly over when I was invited to write *The Best Party of Our Lives*. I hadn't had time to reflect on my Wedding Crasher experience before grad school started, and I was excited for the opportunity. The first task was to find couples who wanted to share their stories, and of course I started with the Wedding Crasher couples. One of the first things I learned when I began talking to newlyweds was that one couple was the first to have a same-sex wedding at the venue where I used to cater. Happily, I imagined them both pinning their boutonnieres to the wall in the grooms' room, or in the brides' room, or both—wherever the hell they wanted.

It is impossible to have a party that expresses the magnitude of love, but to me it seems like the parties people throw for love (a.k.a. weddings) are generally the best ones imaginable—parties whose special nature is palpable even to strangers. This book is a celebration of these transporting, unifying events and the human need to publicly honor love, a rite that should be available to everyone, regardless of their sexual orientation or gender expression.

---

*This book is for all the couples who had to wait too long to marry, for all of those still waiting, for all the great loves that have had to remain hidden, and for every unsuspecting person just going about their day who's about to fall in love right now.*

---

**PART I**

# Engagement

# SURPRISES

## Nick & Spike

NICK HAD NO IDEA THAT THE Craigslist ad he posted in search of a partner for strip-Bananagrams would yield the love of his life. Spike was looking through the ads one day and couldn't resist responding to Nick's hilarious invitation, but he never heard back. Neither of them realized this had been their first interaction until they looked through their e-mail months later; shy Nick had been the type to post Craigslist ads and not follow up on them. This thwarted game of adult Bananagrams must have been destiny—Nick and Spike soon noticed each other on OkCupid and made plans to go on a date. Nick was attending Reed College in Oregon at the time, and Spike worked at a nearby toy store. They went to Nick's improv show in Portland and then to a bar called the Delta. The bar served only beer, which Spike hates, so Nick bought him a Sprite. They ended up talking in Reed's student union building for hours, mostly about their shared aversions and pet peeves (which in their case include actual pets). "We agreed we don't like pets," said Nick, "and that chips are just for the purpose of getting salsa into your mouth." "Which I may have said just to impress him," Spike added. They sat on a sunken couch in the student union building talking until all of the lights went off.

Having just returned from volunteering at a summer camp for children affected by HIV, Spike felt like the date with Nick was a reward from the universe for helping others. It was the first of many such nights—they'd start talking about board games or snacks and suddenly it'd be three in the morning. Soon they were staying most nights either in Nick's narrow dorm bed, where six-foot-nine Spike would usually end up on the radiator, or the huge sagging bed at Spike's, which sucked both of them into it like a marshmallow. In case you're wondering, they finally did end up playing that promised game of strip-Bananagrams.

Many afternoons were spent on Portland's 75 bus, traversing the increasingly familiar distance between each other's homes. That year, Nick came to Spike's family's Thanksgiving and was introduced not only to Spike's parents but also to his aunts, uncles, cousins, and extended family. That spring, Nick graduated from Reed. In the midst of postcollege contentment, the couple was confronted with some big questions. Nick had applied to economics PhD programs in several different states. They had to decide whether they would move together, attempt a long-distance relationship, or break up.

Spike had lived outside the state once before, while attending American University in Washington, DC. He grew up in the small town of The Dalles, Oregon, which had an aluminum plant, a lumber factory, and a railroad-tie factory when he was growing up. Now its most notable industry is Google. Spike described, with amusement, how The Dalles was affected when Google moved in: "We got a Home Depot and our first porn shop, which people protested for like a month."

When Spike was a kid, his mom was executive director of the chamber of commerce, and his dad and grandpa were partners at the lumber company. He had been accepted to Cornish College of the Arts in Seattle for acting when he was eighteen, but had to wait to enroll until finances permitted, because the lumber company burned down shortly after his admittance.

Nick, on the other hand, grew up in Arcata, California, which he described as a "typical small hippie town." His parents, a therapist and a repairman of copiers, typewriters, and printers, moved to California in the '70s and built a yurt. The family is culturally Jewish but not really religious.

Nick was certain he wanted to go to grad school—he was well suited for economics and wanted to use his skills to improve the education system through research and policy work. He had no reservations about leaving Portland, but something was happening to him that had never happened before. Nick had always been the sort of person who could happily go days, even weeks, alone. "You know how they say people in solitary confinement go crazy? That never made sense to me," he explained. For the first time in his life, he found himself really missing another person's company. He wanted to be with Spike, whether they were playing erotic board games or cleaning the gutters or sitting on the couch doing nothing, just because Spike's presence made him happy.

The ever-sociable Spike, however, had always loved the company of others and had long dreamed of pairing off. In fact, he had fantasized about his wedding since he was a kid. He'd watched more romantic comedies than he could count, and a glimpse of a cute guy on the bus was enough to inspire daydreams of color-coordinated linens and boutonnieres. "I was going through my preordained wedding plans, with Nick plugged into my dotted lines," Spike recalled, "and then I thought, I don't know if Nick will even like that. It stopped me in my tracks. I realized he was a person who had opinions. I wasn't just thinking, 'He would look so cute in a tuxedo.'"

It was as if they had traveled a great distance from two different directions and found themselves together in the middle. Though their experiences of love could be described as polar opposites, at a certain point they knew they were in love for the first time, with each other. Spike decided he would go with Nick wherever grad school took him. Nick moved in with Spike for his remaining months in Portland.

As evidenced by the discussion of pets on their first date, Nick and Spike tend to bond more over what they dislike than what they like. "Recently we were watching a cat litter commercial," Spike said, "and we both thought, how terrible to be an adult and to have your concern be your house smelling like cat shit." After they moved in together, Spike was amused when he noticed a Magic: The Gathering Master card in Nick's wallet, identifying Nick not only as a Magic enthusiast, but a sort of Magic scholar. He found out that Nick was referred to as a Magic expert in several online forums. This led to a mostly failed attempt at swapping hobbies: Spike played a few games of Magic, and Nick, who doesn't watch much TV, tried to get into *Buffy the Vampire Slayer*. They both found the failure of this experiment funny, but occasionally their differing tastes can cause real conflict. Spike likes oldies and musical soundtracks (he did end up getting that degree in theater from Cornish College of the Arts), but Nick will listen to any music at all just for a new experience. He is as adventurous as any music collector you'll meet, buying dollar tapes from garage sales out of curiosity. Once, Spike dismissed the music Nick was listening to as "just noise," and Nick became furious. "It was maybe the angriest I've ever seen him," said Spike. "I didn't realize it was representative of a bigger experience for him."

For people so different from each other, a relationship is a continuous process of learning to understand and respect each other's passions. Introverted, analytical Nick's love manifests itself differently than emotional, theatrical Spike's. Growing up, Nick thought about romance but hardly ever about marriage. They had been together for two years when Spike asked Nick to propose to him. Nick knew this was a moment Spike had dreamed of since childhood, so he took his time and thought carefully about it. He found several engagement rings online that looked as if they'd appeal to Spike—a difficult task, since there were few engagement rings in sizes or styles well suited for men. To ensure Spike really loved the ring, Nick decided to wait until after he had proposed and invite Spike to choose from the selection he had found. He needed some kind of ring to make a traditional proposal, though, so he went down to the historic Pike Place Market on Seattle's waterfront and picked out a ring from a junk shop.

Nick and Spike had recently moved to an apartment with a beautiful rooftop deck overlooking the city—a perfect place to propose. But on the evening Nick finally felt ready, it was raining hard by the time he got home from work. He was disappointed but resolved to do it the following week. Once again, as soon as he was home, it began to rain. Spike is the sort of person who strips down to his underwear and gets on his laptop as soon as he's home, making a trip to a cold, rainy rooftop even less appealing. Again, Nick waited. When it rained again the *third* night he planned to propose, he decided he would get Spike up to the deck the next night no matter what. Indeed, it rained the fourth time.

Determined but a little panicked, Nick said the first thing that came to mind: "Let's go up to the roof. We've never seen it in the rain." Spike was tired from work and initially a bit confused by Nick's insistence but agreed to put some pants on and go up to the deck. They looked out together at the lights of the city through the rain, and then Nick pulled Spike close to him. Spike thought his boyfriend was holding him to keep him warm until Nick took out the junk-shop ring. For a moment the whole world beyond that wet rooftop was forgotten. Neither cared that it was raining. After all the thought Nick had put into the proposal, the two could probably have been entirely naked in a garbage truck and it still would have felt like a scene from a movie.

Spike was touched that Nick had picked out several engagement rings for him to choose from, but he only wanted the ring Nick first gave him. To him it represented the tenderness and thoughtfulness of every aspect of Nick's proposal, and he wore it until it turned green and broke. He still has it, in a keepsake box.

Nick's and Spike's families were thrilled when they called that night to announce their engagement—Spike's mom was so excited she immediately posted "Wooooooo!!!"

on all three of their Facebook pages, causing a few people to guess the big news before the couple could announce it themselves.

"How long did you take to plan your wedding?" is of course a funny question for Spike, who was likely staging weddings in the sandbox with his G.I. Joes at the age of five, but the actual amount of time between the engagement and the wedding was about nineteen months. Spike's parade of ideas (as well as those of his mom, who has actually worked as a wedding planner) was a bit of a relief to Nick. Spike discussed every idea with Nick, and only a few (including a Moonstruck truffle for every guest and a drag show at the reception) were vetoed.

As you might expect, a guy pursuing a PhD in economics isn't bad with money. Nick helped bring ideas to fruition that might otherwise have been confined to Spike's Pinterest, like the mismatched silverware for the reception, which they gathered from various Goodwills rather than paying rental prices. The couple avoided decisions about something that could have started a fight—the music at the reception—by putting a space on every RSVP card for one song request. This produced a mix that was eclectic enough for Nick but included plenty of Spike's favorites.

Spike and Nick held their ceremony in an ivy-laced corner of downtown Seattle's Freeway Park (which is much more picturesque than its name makes it sound) that Spike discovered by accident while walking home from work one day. The couple read the vows they wrote for each other on an angular cement fountain that resembled a waterfall. Nick's and Spike's parents recited lyrics of the song "Origin of Love" from the musical *Hedwig and the Angry Inch*, and then the couple stepped on a glass together in the Jewish tradition, to cheers of "mazel tov!"

After the ceremony, the wedding guests were shuttled to Melrose Market Studios. Nick's and Spike's families had spent the day decorating the elegant industrial space with candles and flower arrangements containing book pages— an homage to "The Book of Love" by the Magnetic Fields, a mutual favorite despite their wildly different musical tastes. Nick and Spike had their first dance to this song. Everyone cried. It was clear while they held each other, turning in slow circles, that whatever they loved about the song individually, the dance meant something to them that was shared.

# PROPOSALS

## Grant & Bradford

ON THE EVE OF THE SUMMER solstice, when it stays light out until ten in Seattle, Grant wanted two things—to break into a private pool and go swimming, and to find a good dance party. He was driving around in search of the right pool when he went by an apartment he considered the most beautiful in town. The blinds of the narrow ivy-draped brick building were usually closed, but on this night, they were open, and there was a party going on inside. Grant, with friends in tow, walked through the open door.

No one questioned his presence—in fact he was already flirting with one guy when he was approached by another, more determined one. This was Bradford. Grant and Bradford talked a little, then danced, until they both felt the inevitable moment approaching when dancing turns into kissing. It's entirely possible to be taken with someone for the wrong reasons and to mistake all kinds of feelings for love, but both Grant and Bradford say the kiss had a certain authenticity to it. "I think anytime you kiss somebody, something in the back of your mind goes 'Is this the one?'"

said Bradford. "It's a romantic-comedy moment. I was feeling those feelings."

Bradford's house, south of the apartment where the solstice party was held, had a big backyard, and he invited Grant to spend the evening there with him later in the week. Throughout the day of their date, more and more of Bradford's friends asked to come by that evening. By the time Grant arrived, all of Bradford's best friends were there. Grant was terribly intimidated.

In addition to his date with Bradford, Grant had recently managed to set up a date with a guy he'd had a crush on for a long time. As it turned out, even when surrounded by good friends of Bradford's who he didn't know, Grant had a better rapport with Bradford than he did with the man he'd admired from afar. So he and Bradford made plans to go dancing on Pride weekend.

For Bradford, who is eight years older than Grant, dating had begun to feel like cultural one-upmanship. He was sick of working so hard to present the best version of himself. He decided to be entirely honest. "I said, 'I'm a recovering drug addict, and I'm really bad with money. The rest is gravy,'" Bradford recalled. "This was like the third time we hung out." To naturally forthcoming Grant, this approach was admirable and appealing. He was smitten; there was really nothing about Bradford that he didn't find attractive. In a boat on Lake Union on the Fourth of July, he started to tell Bradford he loved him. "I know what you're going to say, and I'm not ready for it," Bradford told him. He wanted to wait until he was certain he could return the feeling with complete sincerity.

They'd been dating for two months when Bradford's dad died. Though Grant was visiting Oregon at the time, he promptly offered to go to the funeral with Bradford. It was a long ride from Atlanta to North Carolina in a car with Bradford's two six-year-old nephews, who wanted nothing less than an interminable road trip to a funeral. In the car, Bradford tore a picture of a butterfly out of a magazine and wrote "I'm glad you're here." He passed the picture to Grant, who smiled silently and held his hand.

Grant was there to hold his hand throughout that difficult trip. Bradford's family knew he was gay, though he'd never brought it up, and they liked Grant immediately. "I don't know how I would have gotten through it without him," said Bradford.

Bradford grew up in La Crosse, Wisconsin. After graduating from the University of Minnesota, he moved to Seattle to do production work for Teatro ZinZanni, a vaudevillian dinner cabaret. He had always loved singing and was fascinated with Weimar-era cabaret and singers like Edith Piaf and Judy Garland. At the theater, he worked with a woman named Liliane Montevecchi, a silver-screen actress who had costarred with Elvis and Marlon Brando, and danced for the legendary Bolshoi Ballet in Moscow. "She's eighty years old and can still hold her leg over her head," said Bradford. She was part of the inspiration for his turbaned French drag persona, Mal DeFleur.

Grant, who grew up in Portland, Oregon, also worked at Teatro ZinZanni but as a props carpenter, though his degree is in English literature and secondary education. He acquired his carpentry skills doing sculpture and installation art. The unlikely venue of Grant's first installation piece was his conservative Christian high school, where an art teacher advocated for him to do a piece critiquing the church in the school's cafeteria. He was stirred by the experience and has been doing installation art ever since. Creative passion is something Grant and Bradford share to an extent they've never known before in a relationship. Sometimes, Brad performs as Mal DeFleur at Grant's art shows. Their biggest disagreements are about art and music, but they generally find their debates about aesthetics enriching.

Bradford and Grant's first real fight was in an IHOP. They were talking about how they relate to their brothers. Suddenly they were so angry they didn't notice their pancakes had arrived. They walked out without eating. Rather than driving them apart, however, the fight made them realize how much they cared about each other. It was what Bradford needed to be certain he was serious about Grant.

A few weeks later under a tree a few blocks from the same pancake house, they agreed they wanted to be boyfriends. Soon after, Grant made Bradford a special gift, a collage with words from one of their favorite Neko Case songs, "I'm an Animal."

Bradford was Grant's first real boyfriend. "I was utterly expanded," Grant said. "I was twenty-two and had come out a year earlier. Bradford was so knowledgeable about gay history and art, and was comfortable being gay in a way I hadn't had modeled for me before." Grant was the first boyfriend Bradford had ever lived with, as Bradford had a rule against moving in before two years, and none of his relationships had lasted that long. When Bradford met Grant, he was battling a drug problem. By his account, it's not the sort of thing one is aware of when it's happening, and it happened very quickly. It materialized with awful suddenness and ended up consuming nearly three years of his life. Three weeks prior to meeting Grant, he promised a good friend that he would either get clean or move home to Wisconsin and start over. His honesty about it with Grant saved their relationship, and perhaps Bradford himself. It was Grant who convinced him to go to treatment. Bradford persevered, Grant graduated from Seattle Pacific University, and they moved into a house together.

Bradford went into their garage so infrequently he didn't notice the disappearance of the garage keys. One night, when they'd lived together about six months, Grant asked Bradford to dress up because he was taking him out for a nice dinner in Georgetown, a Seattle neighborhood. Bradford thought this was odd, since he knew that neighborhood well and couldn't think of any restaurants there that required ties. He assumed they must be going to a friend's house. Things became odder when they arrived at their destination, a darkened parking lot outside an abandoned warehouse, which appeared empty. It definitely wasn't a restaurant. Inside, a tile path surrounded by candles snaked into a dark room. As he entered, Bradford heard the first notes of the song "Origin of Love" from *Hedwig and the Angry Inch*. The music seemed to come from all around.

In recent months, Grant had been in their garage whenever Bradford was away, constructing an art installation that followed the narrative of the song. As the story goes, the gods, fearing the power of a race of two-headed proto-humans (including Children of the Sun, made of two men; Children of the Earth, made of two women; and Children of the Moon, made of a man and a woman) split them in half and scattered them, leaving the halves perpetually in search of each other. Along the candle-lit path, Brad found sculptures of wood, metal, and paper, representing each verse of the song. He was in awe. He hadn't a clue what Grant had been up to, and he walked through the installation as if through a dream. At the end of the path, he opened a glittering circular door to find Grant in a room illuminated by candles and a box of glowing words that read "The Origin of Love." Grant was holding a ring and proposed. Grant then produced a second ring, saying "If you want to propose to me now, you can."

"I'm somebody who likes to think things through, have a conversation about them," Bradford said. "I was like, oh gosh, I have to make a decision. I don't think my brain has ever moved so fast." They'd had favorable discussions about marriage, but those discussions were vague. For a moment, Bradford was paralyzed. He looked around the work of art Grant had created as an invitation to spend their lives together, realizing that something inside Grant made him passionate and determined enough to invest hundreds of pounds of wood and metal and many hours of labor into this project, and he had faith in their love. He saw Grant's vision of beauty and knew he wanted that in his life forever. "Bradford dropped to his knee and delivered the most gorgeous, present, and eloquent proposal of all time," Grant said.

The only people who knew Grant was building an installation for the proposal were his family, who loved Bradford and shared Grant's anticipation. Bradford noticed his family and close friends had always taken their relationship especially seriously. Shortly after, they went into the bar where their friend Amelia worked and simultaneously knelt to ask her to officiate their wedding, which cracked her up. She agreed, of course.

Grant and Bradford's biggest obstacle in planning the wedding was simply the number of people they wanted to invite. The invitations numbered over two hundred. Though their wedding was black tie, they hoped to capture the atmosphere of their favorite neighborhood gay bars at the reception, so they asked friends Marcus and Jodi to deejay.

Grant made another installation for the wedding—1,422 jars, one for every day they had spent together, threaded together to create an enormous beaded curtain. Their mothers walked them down the aisle to "I'm an Animal," the song whose lyrics Grant had collaged on the first gift he ever gave Bradford. The words read, "There are things that I'm still so afraid of, but my courage is roaring like the sound of the sun."

# RINGS

---

## *Ann & Sheri*

THE PIKE PLACE MARKET'S COBBLESTONE streets and narrow alleys are lined with boutiques, century-old bars, and vendors of produce and flowers from nearby farms. In 1975, Ann opened a specialty foods store in the market. She sold imported goods and bulk food; it was one of the few places in town one could find a fifty-five-gallon drum of olive oil at the time.

Sheri lived in Wenatchee, Washington, and frequently biked over the pass in the Cascade Mountains to shop in the market. As soon as she discovered Ann's shop, she became a regular. "Ann got me to buy a gallon of olive oil and twenty pounds of pasta every time I came over!" said Sheri. On one such visit, Ann mentioned to Sheri that she'd just bought a house nearby, and her tub was broken. "I know how to fix tubs!" Sheri told her, even though she'd never been near a broken tub. Somehow, knowing nothing about plumbing, Sheri fixed it easily. "I thought, that's what I need," said Ann, grinning. "A hausfrau."

Ann was giddy when Sheri invited her to Wenatchee, where they went hiking, climbing, and out for pizza. "Ann is a world-class climber," said Sheri. On their fourth date, Ann planned to make Sheri a big Italian dinner. When Sheri came by Ann's work to pick her up, she overheard someone say, "She's going to be crushed when she hears what happened to Ann." Ann was riding her bike down the Counterbalance, a hill better suited for mountaineers than cyclists, on her way to work, and something caught in her spokes, sending her flying. She wound up in the hospital with a fractured spine. Sheri was on her way to the hospital before Ann's coworkers had even finished their account of what happened.

Sheri met Ann's mom, dad, and brother in the hospital. As soon as Sheri was acquainted with Ann's family, love and concern for Ann brought them together. "After the accident, I realized life is precious," said Sheri. Ann was unable to walk for three months following the accident, so Sheri moved in to care for her. She found a nursing job at the University of Washington. There wasn't much deliberation about the move—Ann and Sheri are one of those rare couples who loved each other almost immediately. Ann says she knew she loved Sheri when she asked her on their first date.

Ann grew up in Seattle, where her big Italian family had resided for three generations. Her family's tradition of working with food inspired her to open a specialty foods store.

"Food, family, funerals, garbage," joked Sheri. "It's the Italian way!" As Ann befriended farmers, artisans, and other shop owners working on the waterfront, Pike Place became like another family for her. She ran her shop there for twenty-five years and remains a member of the PDA (Pike Place Market Preservation & Development Authority) Council. "Before Whole Foods existed, that was my gig," said Ann.

Sheri grew up in Minneapolis, then lived in Colorado for a while before a nursing job brought her to Wenatchee. She had always loved hiking, canoeing, and the arts, and while Wenatchee offered plenty of opportunities to enjoy the first two of these, there wasn't much of the third. Sheri first ventured into Seattle for this reason. She is an avid guitarist—the first present Ann gave her was a guitar.

Sheri knew Ann loved cycling but guessed she would be afraid to get back on a bike after the accident. When Ann could walk again, Sheri gave her a new bicycle and gentle encouragement to resume doing a thing that made her happy despite her traumatic experience with it.

That Christmas, shortly after Ann had recovered, Sheri gave her another present—two rings set with moonstones she bought from a jewelry maker in Pike Place. The couple was sharing a quiet Christmas Eve dinner when Sheri showed Ann the rings. She asked Ann to be with her for life. Ann of course agreed. There was no thought about the legal institution of marriage—neither thought their marriage would be officially recognized, and at the time, neither of them cared. Though they'd hardly been together a year, in the wake of the accident they realized the feelings they'd had when they met weren't a passing fancy. The bike crash forced the two to imagine what life without each other would be like, and neither of them wanted that life.

Thus began Ann and Sheri's happy (essentially) married life. When asked what they most like to do together, Ann promptly replied, "Everything!" "That's sweet," said Sheri. They especially enjoy climbing, hiking, riding bikes, and cooking. "Sheri's a fabulous chef," said Ann. "She just made a delicious pumpkin pasta dish. Brussels sprouts on the side." This is high praise considering the role of food in Ann's professional life and family history.

Ann and Sheri are also both fans of poetry and theater, and recalled with amusement a night they went to the Alice B. Theatre, which was founded in 1984 with Seattle's first gay and lesbian theater festival. They went to Alice B. regularly, their favorite show being the annual "Christmas Nightmare," where members of the audience were invited to tell the tale of their worst Christmas ever. Alice B. also had a show where couples got on stage and answered trivia questions about each other. The night Ann and Sheri decided to showcase their relationship trivia skills, they couldn't remember a thing about each other. When someone asked how long they had been together, one of them answered, "Twenty years." The audience was stunned, and then laughed. They may not be so good at remembering each other's favorite foods or movies, but the reason they have a hard time remembering fights is because there have been so few—their nieces and nephews consider them role models for healthy relationships and go to them for advice.

It had been another thirteen years when DOMA was overturned, and Ann and Sheri decided to get married for legal benefits. "It's always been like we were married," said Ann. They felt, as well they should, that a thirty-three-year relationship deserved a party, and they began to plan a wedding. Naturally, they wanted to get married at Pike Place Market, where they had met and had gotten their wedding rings, but no one had ever held a wedding there before. "When Annie gets an idea, nothing stops her," said Sheri. "So we were thinking of a fun venue—we wanted to have a party. I kept thinking of places like the Arboretum. She said, hey, let's see if we can get married at the market. The market said sure, why not and offered huge support."

On their wedding day, Ann and Sheri had a ceremony at the Pike Place Market Goodwin Library overlooking the market filled with visitors, vendors, and flowers. The wedding ceremony was attended exclusively by family and close friends, including some family members who flew in from the East Coast. Ann's niece Olivia was their officiant.

Ann's niece Maggie spoke on her behalf, Sheri's brother on her behalf, and Sheri's nephew Evan recited a Tennyson poem. "Evan is so shy, but he did it!" said Sheri. Mountains of daffodils from a vendor in the market were an ideal decoration for a wedding in March. Oddly (for clammy Seattle), it was eighty degrees that day.

Their rings still held the moonstones Sheri had bought at Pike Place during their first winter together. Ann and Sheri had their wedding rings for so long that the metal wore out, so they took the moonstones and had them reset in gold bands. They're still friends with the maker of their original rings. "We see him around," said Ann. "I think he lives on Orcas Island now."

Immediately after the wedding ceremony, Ann and Sheri rushed down to help close off the entire Joe Desimone Bridge (a covered bridge connecting the upper and lower levels of the market) for their reception dance party. The batting and heaters they had rented were never used—the evening was balmy. When the sun went down, they discovered that the Ferris wheel on the waterfront glowed with rainbow lights, a happy coincidence. The reception party filled the bridge and lasted late into the night. Strangers sneaked in just to dance.

When a friend of Ann and Sheri's took off her fancy high-heeled shoes so she could dance, a passing stranger tried to take them. Fortunately, a security guard saw him, and told the would-be shoe thief, "I don't think those will fit." His response was, "Yeah, but they're so sexy!" Nothing like that reception had ever happened at Pike Place before, only a few hundred feet from the shop where Ann and Sheri met. "There were friends, neighbors, the market community, people we've met in our travels," said Ann. "The market community is our home. It was us saying thank you for the people who have supported us."

# PART II

# Planning

# BUDGETS

IN 2006, ALYSON WAS STUDYING HISTORY and political science in Great Falls, Montana. Having grown up in Montana, she belonged to a LiveJournal group devoted to the state. She found there was one woman in the group whose posts she enjoyed more than anyone else's. This was Carolina. They struck up a conversation online, and it turned out the admiration was mutual. Carolina didn't grow up in Montana, but she had lived there for seven years, and her thoughts about the place resonated with Alyson. For months they talked online every day, about anything and everything, finding one thing after another in common and laughing at each other's jokes even though they were alone in their rooms. Eventually, though, due to the busyness and turbulence of life, and because they lived so far from each other that visiting was impractical, they lost touch.

Two years later, Carolina found Alyson on Facebook, and their conversations resumed with renewed energy. They often talked late into the night. "We talked a lot on the phone," said Alyson. "We had so much in common—feminism, queer stuff, *Buffy*." Carolina had just gotten out of a terrible relationship and couldn't believe how much better conversation felt with Alyson than with her ex. They were attracted to each other but so nervous to make a move that they remained best friends for some time. They confessed their feelings over the phone on July 15, 2008, about two months after they reconnected. The conversation began tentatively at first, but by the end of it, they were discussing marriage and children.

At the time, they could have had them together—Alyson is a transgender woman. She grew up in Montana in a relatively conservative family, but when, at sixteen, she told her father she was experiencing confusion about her gender, he was surprisingly sensitive and receptive. At twenty-two, though, when Alyson came out to both her parents as transgender (having discovered the nature of her confusion), her mother's crushing response was that God makes no mistakes and that she would make an ugly woman anyway. "I basically went back in the closet for nine years," said Alyson. She moved to Spokane for the first three years of college and then back to Montana where she earned a degree in history and political science at her hometown's university. At the time, she considered herself an introvert. She was shy and depressed.

Carolina had known Alyson was trans since they had met on LiveJournal, where she went by a female name and pronouns, even before she was out as trans in her daily life, except to a few people. "Carolina knew I was trans going into our relationship," said Alyson. "I'd been using my name online for a good three years before we met. She always used the correct pronouns."

Carolina's upbringing may have laid the foundation for her sensitivity and open-mindedness. She was raised in San Francisco by two lesbians who were co-parents but weren't in a romantic relationship. She lived in Michigan and Montana before moving to Seattle on a whim. After working in retail for years, she now attends Seattle Central Community College, getting her prerequisites for a degree from the University of Washington in gender, women, and sexuality studies.

In July of 2008, soon after the phone conversation during which they first said they loved each other, Alyson moved to Missoula, where Carolina was living at the time. Carolina was living not only with her ex, who she was not on the best terms with, but her ex's unbearable mom, who had moved in with them several months before.

Miraculously, the circumstances of Alyson and Carolina's first date in person did nothing to diminish their excitement about each other. The date consisted of Alyson, Carolina, and Carolina's ex going to see a horror movie starring Kiefer Sutherland called *Mirrors*, which Alyson and Carolina both hated. Alyson's delicate description of the experience was "awkward."

Shortly afterward, Carolina's ex's mom kicked her out of the house in a fit. Fortunately, Alyson found Carolina a room in the hotel where she was working, where they stayed together for a month. It was a brutal time for both of them, Carolina having lost her home and any hope of an amicable breakup, and Alyson having recently lost a grandmother she was close with. They learned what a comfort they were to each other when things went to hell. They had been together six or seven months, but they agree they really became a couple during that month. They've lived together ever since. As things settled down (moving from a hotel to an actual apartment was a relief), they began to notice the shared enjoyment of many small things that made living together so comfortable—the Beatles, stuffed animals, black licorice.

The following year Alyson and Carolina moved to California together. Despite being newly in love and happy to be in Carolina's company, Alyson suffered increasingly from depression and social anxiety. She knew she was a woman, but largely because of her parents' refusal to accept her, she was afraid to present herself as she truly was. It was hard for her to wear the clothing that reflected her identity in public, and the thought of actually transitioning (which for her entailed going through hormone therapy) seemed an impossible dream.

It was Carolina who finally convinced Alyson to face her fears. "She was going to leave me if I didn't transition," said Alyson. "Why marry someone who's miserable and depressed?" They moved to Seattle partly because of the city's excellent social services, which made the expensive process much easier. Alyson and Carolina had planned to get married since that day in July when they'd first said they loved each other, but they decided to wait until Alyson adjusted to the transition before making another big change in their lives.

They found jobs at drugstores just a few blocks from each other on Mercer Island. Competing drugstores, actually—Carolina worked at Rite Aid and Alyson worked at Walgreens. Though the managers at Walgreens and a couple of other employees knew Alyson was trans, she requested to be transferred to another location when she began hormone treatment. The process was already scary enough for her—she did not want the added stress of switching from male to female clothing and pronouns at work. She introduced herself as a woman at a new job for the first time.

Her appearance changed remarkably as a result of the hormones—she passed easily as a woman and was finally able to wear the clothing she felt comfortable in. Though Carolina had always been supportive of her, Alyson worried her physical changes might affect Carolina's attraction to her. To the contrary, Carolina had always known her as a woman and could see that the person emerging as she transitioned was the person she really was. It was as if Carolina could see the person she had always loved with increasing clarity. As Alyson's confidence increased, she became happier and more outgoing. Having previously been uncomfortable around nearly everyone, she was surprised by how social she became.

The morning following Seattle Pride in 2013, after a five-year engagement, Alyson and Carolina woke up knowing it was time to get married. All the elements they had been working for were in place—they had steady jobs and a home together, and Alyson was finally able to openly live as a woman. They wanted to have the wedding two weeks later, on July 15, the anniversary of the day they said they loved each other for the first time.

With the date of the wedding so near, they didn't have time to save money—they had to figure out a way to do it for about $300. Alyson's parents knew and liked Carolina but hadn't seen Alyson since she started hormones. In the interest of keeping their celebration free of drama, they decided not to tell Alyson's parents. Carolina's moms were delighted to hear about the wedding, though only one of them could attend. She and her wife bought all the food and drinks for the occasion—a vegetable platter, dips, and wine from PCC, the local natural market, and cupcakes from Carolina and Alyson's favorite bakery, Trophy. A friend of Alyson's from work was ordained in order to officiate them.

Alyson's wedding dress was a hand-me-down she'd worn at Pride the year she and Carolina became engaged. Carolina's dress, as well as the bracelets they chose to exchange in place of rings, were from Macy's.

The morning of the wedding, Carolina and Alyson went for pedicures with a couple of friends, stopped at Taco Time, then headed home in time for guests to arrive. They held the ceremony in their backyard, with the few friends who happened to be free on a Monday afternoon. "We told everyone else we'll have a big reception in a couple years—don't worry about it," said Alyson. The gathering was quiet and comfortable. The ceremony itself only lasted about five minutes. The day was just as Carolina and Alyson had wanted it. A photographer friend of theirs took pictures for free, as a wedding gift, and they used one of her photos for their holiday card, which they sent to all of their friends and family, even the less accepting of them. The photo is the first of Carolina and Alyson as a married couple, and among the first of them as two women together.

# GUESTS

## Jeffrey & Rodney

IN 1992, RODNEY WAS STAYING IN a hotel in downtown Seattle that no longer exists. He had just moved from San Francisco and didn't know anyone in town yet. In a pizza shop, he combed the personal ads in the *Stranger* for an interesting date. He only highlighted two ads, one of which read, "I'm a thirty-three-year-old bearded bear. These excite me: salsa, wrestling, biceps, Jean Genet, lesbians, tattoos, short guys, James Brown, the ocean, hiking." This was how he met Jeffrey, who, as it turned out, had also responded to the other ad Rodney highlighted, which yielded the worst date of Jeffrey's life.

The two went out for coffee and wound up hanging out into the evening. Jeffrey was charmed, and Rodney was entirely swept off his feet by Jeffrey and his tour of the city. His limited experience of romance with men added to the thrill. Rodney had always been out in what he described as "a classic '80s androgynous, bisexual way." He did sort of a genderfuck thing, wearing hippie peasant dresses and going to punk shows. Rodney preferred house parties to gay bars.

When Rodney spoke dismissively of the punk bands he played guitar with in his teens and twenties, Jeffrey said, "He actually plays beautifully."

Rodney was born on an air force base in Florida. His parents divorced when he was seven, and his mom married a former stuntman for '60s westerns with two ex-wives and nine children. When Rodney's stepdad decided he wanted to run fishing-boat tours, Rodney's mom sold their house. The entire family wound up living on a powerboat. "The fishing boat tours never came to be. The public harbor where we were moored wouldn't allow people to live on their boats, so we all lived in a hotel room at one point," said Rodney. Family conflict motivated Rodney to run away from home at seventeen. He got into the University of Tampa on a creative-writing scholarship and majored in zoology. He now teaches sustainable horticulture at Edmonds Community College.

Jeffrey grew up in Sacramento, California. "I was the baby of the family in stereotypical ways," he said. "Shy but funny, creative, wanted to become an artist." His creativity eventually led him to art college. He met an older man named Amador who was a high school teacher. They had to be somewhat secretive about their relationship, though, because of the Briggs Initiative, which made it legal to fire teachers for being gay. They had been together nine years, essentially living as a married couple, when Amador succumbed to AIDS. Jeffrey was shocked when Amador's family, who he believed he was on good terms with, took their house and many of their mutually owned possessions. As if this wasn't enough, they had Jeffrey's name removed from the obituary. He could have gotten over the house and the stuff, but the removal of his name from the obituary was unforgivable. So many years later, the pain still returns when he talks about it.

Rodney was the first person Jeffrey dated seriously after Amador. They quickly found that when they did nearly anything together, it was more fun. Both of them were, as Jeffrey put it, "as musically promiscuous as you can get" and were excited to explore each other's tastes. One of the first things that attracted Jeffrey to Rodney was his excitement about things he didn't know. Rodney had an extensive knowledge of blues and punk, whereas Jeffrey was more familiar with experimental music, musicals, and disco. Rodney was impressed that Jeffrey was a member of the original Patti Smith fan club.

Jeffrey took Rodney to see musicals and experimental theater, and Rodney took Jeffrey to rock clubs. They met during the heyday of grunge in Seattle, when there was a potentially memorable show nearly every night of the week. Together, they altered anti-homosexuality Chick tracts, conservative Christian comics, making them into pornographic pro-gay parodies. They dispensed these pamphlets (which they called "Chick-with-a-Dick Publications") all over the city, just as conservative religious groups did with Chick tracts. When they weren't scattering homoerotic confetti, they went out to eat, most frequently at a restaurant called Sea Garden, where they usually ordered squid. (Jeffrey now has an orange squid tattoo curled around his forearm—the two consider squid a kind of mascot of their relationship.) Over many dinners, they found they agreed about a variety of political and ethical issues. At the time, they both considered themselves anarchists, though Jeffrey now leans more toward socialism. "During the AIDS crisis, when my partner died, [I] was radicalized," Jeffrey said.

Neither of them said there was a specific moment when they realized they were in love, but Rodney remembered one morning, while they were camping, when his love for Jeffrey struck him with particular intensity. He woke up to find a buck standing beside their tent, as if out of a mythical scene. "I thought, what a wonderful life I've found myself in," said Rodney. "It's gradual, but you can point to moments when you're getting stitched into it. You keep adding the stitches that bind you together."

"I'm resistant to words like love because they're so ambiguous," said Jeffrey. "People don't articulate what they're really feeling. I remember when I realized I knew I wanted to tell him I loved him, and I had some trepidation." Though their relationship has had its difficulties, the moments that remind Jeffrey why he loves Rodney have been continuous.

In 1994, Jeffrey and Rodney became registered domestic partners with the City of Seattle, on the first day that the city offered domestic partner registration. National media was there, and unbeknownst to Rodney and Jeffrey, they ended up in nationally broadcast video clips. They were surprised when they got congratulatory calls from family later that evening.

Around the time they met, a niece of Jeffrey's had a baby. "A little while later she had another one," said Jeffrey. "They became our de facto sons." Jeffrey and Rodney loved those kids so much that they eventually wanted a child of their own. They decided to adopt a teenager, because older children are the hardest to place in foster families and so their child would be the same age as their niece's kids— essentially an adopted brother. Their son, Chris, was fifteen when they adopted him. Chris had a rough past, but Jeffrey and Rodney were determined to provide a stable and loving home. The three went to counseling together as he adjusted to his new life.

When same-sex marriage became legal in Oregon in 2004, Jeffrey and Rodney went to Portland to get married at the first opportunity. They and another couple, who had flown in from New York for the same purpose, took turns witnessing each other's marriages. When they returned to Seattle, they had a big, classic reception party, with friends, family, and co-workers. They had been together eleven years.

Having married for political reasons as much as for love, they were irate when the marriage was nullified after a week when the state went back on its decision. They got a rebate check for sixty dollars in the mail. For Jeffrey, this brought back the rage he'd felt after suffering at the hands of the state when his first partner died. He would only refer to Rodney as his nullified husband.

They had to wait another twelve years before Referendum 74 passed in Washington. They decided not to tell anyone they were getting married, because they didn't want anyone to be upset that they weren't invited and because Jeffrey hated the way his straight acquaintances talked for months about their approaching weddings when he'd been with someone he loved and couldn't marry for over twenty years.

They wanted their wedding to be not just a celebration of their relationship but a family day. "Family day came about because we were reaching the deadline for our domestic partnership to automatically turn into a marriage, and we realized it was right before the anniversary of the day we adopted our son," said Jeffrey. "It seemed like a fitting way to make it 'legal,' since we had to make it legal for Chris to be our son as well. Rodney thought of it. I didn't have to think twice about it. We asked our son and he agreed. It just seemed natural." They had many other family members from out of town who would have loved to attend, but as important as those people are to Jeffrey and Rodney, they just wanted a tiny party for themselves and their son—a celebration of the home they had created together.

They invited only five guests to their second wedding— their son, Chris (who now, legally, was both Jeffrey and Rodney's son—whereas before Rodney had been designated the "primary parent," a standard practice for same-sex adoptions prior to the passage of Referendum 74); their dog, Aspen; Rodney's good friends Julie and Amy whom he met in grad school; and their daughter, Sophie. Amy and Julie had been together eight years, and Jeffrey and Rodney had attended their wedding as well. Amy and Julie brought flowers and champagne; Sophie was their flower girl. On the bank of a little creek, they lit two ceremonial candles in a cast-iron holder, improvised their vows, and exchanged rings. Afterward they had dinner at a restaurant they'd had date nights at for twenty years. Besides the triumph of getting something they had dreamed of for years that had always just barely eluded them, Jeffrey and Rodney's wedding day wasn't much different than any other day—the simple things they like to do made more enjoyable by each other's company and the company of people they love.

# BACHELORETTE PARTIES

## Lauren & Kristin

WHILE ON SUMMER VACATION FROM Oberlin College, Lauren worked at a Girl Scout camp just outside of Seattle. While getting settled into her cabin, she was introduced to Kristin, another camp counselor. Lauren assumed she wouldn't like Kristin, because she resembled the cliquey popular girls she remembered from high school with her model-worthy looks and the black North Face jacket that had been ubiquitous among the cool kids. Kristin seemed like the sort of person who was very pretty but not very nice. They worked together all summer but never had a real conversation until camp was nearly over. When they did, Lauren found Kristin quite likeable, and Kristin returned the sentiment—more than Lauren realized at the time. Later, Lauren was amused to discover that Kristin had been the only person at her high school who owned a black North Face jacket. "It was warm for hiking!" said Kristin.

When camp ended, they were eager to continue their friendship. They decided to take a short trip to Cannon Beach in Oregon, a tiny seaside town known for its proximity to dramatic rock formations created by ancient volcanoes. Kristin and Lauren drank hot cocoa and watched the original *Robin Hood* with Errol Flynn. They now describe the trip as a date that only Kristin was aware of as such. Later, when Lauren recognized what was happening, she felt giddy and overwhelmingly anxious. Lauren had never really dated—she simply had no interest. At twenty, she was beginning to wonder why this was and to worry about it. The previous year, she had pursued a guy in college, but when he responded with affection, she became nervous and avoided him.

In high school, Lauren's mother, who had said she would accept her regardless of any sexual orientation (by coincidence, her mom's and dad's best friends are both gay women), had asked her if she was gay, but she declined to answer. At Oberlin, her roommate asked her out. Panicked, Lauren pretended she hadn't heard her. "It was the reaction of a twelve-year-old," said Lauren. "It was awful."

At Cannon Beach, though, Lauren felt the familiar terror when she realized Kristin had a crush on her, but it was quickly overcome by a kind of desire she had never experienced. "I had never had that kind of connection before," she said. "A few months later, I loved her." Back at Oberlin, she mentioned that she was dating a woman to the roommate who had asked her out the year before, and she asked Lauren why it had taken her so long to figure it out. "I didn't want to be a poser," Lauren said. "I didn't want to just say I was a lesbian, because lesbians arc cool." To which her roommate replied, "You're *such* a lesbian. No one thinks lesbians are cool." [Author's note: it was because of this exchange that I learned the term "lug" (lesbian until graduation) and Oberlin's reputation for them.]

Several of the girls considered cool at Girl Scout camp were openly gay, which may have reinforced the idea. Kristin had actually dated as little as Lauren when they met, but it was because no one at her high school really dated. Kristin grew up in Woodinville, Washington, (a small town north of Seattle) and was attending University of Puget Sound when she met Lauren. Kristin's family's only worry when they found out she was with a woman was that there would be no grandkids. Kristin, who had always wanted children, explained to her mom that it was still quite possible. "She was like, oh, well that's fine then!" Kristin said.

Lauren, who grew up in Portland, Oregon, encountered small resistance from her family when they realized a serious relationship would decrease her presence at family game nights. "When I came out to my parents, they were neither surprised nor impressed," she said.

Because she and Kristin were both in college, their relationship was long distance for the next three years. They're now thankful their prior relationship experience was so limited—these years were easier because they didn't yet know how much they would enjoy living together. Lauren didn't hesitate to move in with Kristin in Seattle as soon as she graduated from Oberlin.

Neither of them had any trepidation about living together—they'd been with each other long enough to have agreed on some key points. They knew that they wanted to live in Seattle, that they wanted kids, and that they wanted to buy a house together when they could. Initially, all they felt was joy—they hadn't even realized how much they'd missed each other during school.

However, sometimes the scariest thing is getting what you want. This fear was the cause of Lauren and Kristin's first fight ever—Lauren simply couldn't believe she had met the person she wanted to marry after so little dating and at such a young age. She was perfectly happy with Kristin but became troubled by hypothetical scenarios in which their relationship limited her freedom. "Like, what if I want to move to DC?" said Lauren. "I didn't, but what if I did?" She panicked and briefly broke up with Kristin.

Kristin's parents had been together for ages, and witnessing everything they'd gone through together shaped her own relationship mentality, which is all about communication and compromise. Once she'd explained to Lauren that the decisions they'd made about their life together weren't set in stone, Lauren relaxed. "I asked her, 'Why do you think I wouldn't move to DC with you?'" she said. They still fight, but the fights are much more manageable now that they know each other better. "I think we fight when we don't talk enough," said Kristin. "If we're not in sync."

Lauren knew that Kristin had wanted to marry her for years but that she was respectfully waiting for Lauren's fears surrounding making the official decision to spend their lives together to subside. They'd lived together for four years when Lauren took the leap. She knew that things wouldn't always be perfect and that they wouldn't always agree, but she was certain she wanted to be with Kristin for the rest of her life. She had learned to trust that her happiness was a priority for Kristin and that Kristin's was for her.

Choosing a ring involved examining a fistful of diamonds in a parking lot to see how they looked in natural light. "The salesperson asked if I wanted to hold them," said Lauren. "I was like, no, are you crazy?" Kristin would probably have been just as happy to receive a Funyun as an engagement ring—Lauren was making her dreams come true.

Soon afterward she took Lauren for a seemingly random, oddly timed walk on Alki Beach in West Seattle. It was early, and Lauren was hungry, so initially she protested. Fortunately, Kristin talked her into it—it was important to her that they were in exactly the right place when she made her own proposal. It was cold that morning, but the miles-long beach, with its view of downtown Seattle and surrounding old-growth forest, would have made for a romantic walk even if Kristin hadn't stopped Lauren to give her a ring. They had breakfast afterward at a famously decadent water-front restaurant, Salty's.

They were so eager to tell their families that when Kristin's parents didn't pick up the phone, they drove to their house in Woodinville and loitered in their driveway until they were home from work. "We tried to convince them we were just in the neighborhood, but you can't really make up a reason for being in Woodinville," said Lauren. "Kristin's mom was like, 'hi, do you have an announcement to make?'"

The wedding took about a year to plan. "The only dif-ference for gay weddings is you decide which traditions to keep," said Kristin. Kristin and Lauren had to make such a decision when choosing their wedding outfits. They didn't want identical dresses, but they didn't want one of the dresses to look more important than the other. They briefly entertained the idea of a suit and dress. "Ellen DeGeneres wore some kind of white linen suit," said Lauren. "But my friend was like, that's crazy—you wear dresses all the time. David Sedaris has this great quote, his answer to the question 'Which one's the guy?' 'We both are! That's what makes us homosexuals!'" They eventually found two dresses they loved—a white dress and a dress in a shade of eggplant, and they had one of the dresses altered so they'd be the same length (to the horror of the elderly Russian women at the tailor shop).

Lauren and Kristin customized their bachelorette party in a similar fashion. They had many mutual friends and envisioned their bachelorette parties about the same way, so rather than two parties, they decided to have one big one. They chose a Mexican restaurant called Peso's for its tasty, voluminous margaritas and (another opinion they share) ridiculously attractive servers. Though she couldn't attend—and probably wouldn't have enjoyed the hot waitstaff as much as they did—Kristin's mom offered to foot the bill.

A few drinks in, one of their friends mentioned that their server looked familiar. Everyone agreed, and it wasn't long before someone figured out she'd been a contestant on *A Shot at Love with Tila Tequila*, a reality TV show on which sixteen straight men and sixteen lesbians competed for Tila's affection. Tila was rumored to have stopped corresponding with the guy who won when the show ended, because she preferred one of the women, but the producers told her whom to choose. The server seemed to think the raucous group was making fun of her when the question "Were you on Tila Tequila?" was followed by "We're having a bachelorette party!" but she wound up sitting down at their table and telling them all about the show. Many more margaritas followed. At the end of the evening, Kristin's mom called and tried to pay the tab over the phone. "They were like, this is a bar, not the Ritz!" said Lauren. "She had to, like, convince them to let her. She's a classy lady. We got to tell everyone, congratulations, your drinks are free!" The server recognized Lauren and Kristin for years afterward and stopped to talk with them on their semi-regular Peso's dates.

The hardest part of planning the wedding, Kristin and Lauren agree, was finding a location. They found that most popular wedding spots were booked a year out, sometimes more. They finally settled on a resort on the Semiahmoo Spit in Blaine, Washington. They drove out to Blaine early with family and friends to decorate the wedding venue with paper ornaments and place markers made of marshmallows for the guests—a homage to the summer they met at Girl Scout camp. The night before the ceremony, their parents threw a party, giving the couple a chance to relax after all the preparation.

Traditionally, the groom isn't allowed to see the bride the day of the wedding, until the ceremony, but as there were no grooms present, Lauren and Kristin helped each other into their wedding gowns (some of their favorite wedding photos are of this moment). They hid together, watching the guests arrive as they nervously rehearsed their vows.

When their three-year-old flower girl, who had been an enthusiastic participant in the rehearsals, spiked her ball of chrysanthemums like a football, their elementary school–aged ring bearer took on her duties as well. Besides this obstacle, which was more adorable than anything else, the only trouble they faced was when the judge who officiated them discovered she wasn't qualified to sign a domestic partnership—only a notary can do so. However, the judge was an eloquent officiant, and the domestic partnership that was made official after the wedding has since transferred into a marriage license.

After they exchanged vows at the end of a long dock, as the August afternoon turned into evening, the couple performed one more wedding ritual that was theirs alone. At Girl Scout camp, beach rocks with stripes that formed unbroken bands encircling the rocks were considered lucky, and a person could wish on one by throwing it into the water. Tossing two rocks off the dock into the water, Kristin and Lauren had the rare opportunity to make a wish at a moment when they both felt they had all they'd ever wished for.

# LOCATIONS

---

## Greg & Larry

IN 1981, GREG AND THE MAN he was dating at the time borrowed a truck from Larry to help them move a refrigerator, and Greg and Larry noticed each other in an idle sort of way. They ran into each other later, after Greg and his boyfriend had broken up, and talked awhile. "I thought he was looking good," Larry recalled with a smile. Soon Larry invited Greg over for dinner at his apartment. He was already smitten with tall, elegant Greg, and he was so nervous about the date that he asked friends what to cook for dinner. He was recommended Stouffer's lasagna, because it makes a simple passage from box to table during which little can go wrong. Larry had no idea at the time that Greg was an excellent cook. He also had no idea how much Greg liked him— enough that he couldn't have cared less about frozen lasagna (though it was partly what inspired him to give Larry pots and pans for Christmas).

Greg had recently finished art school at the University of Washington. He had been passionate about art since he started going to galleries as a teenager, but by the time he graduated from UW, he was coming to terms with the fact that he wasn't much of an artist himself. Rather than becoming discouraged, he thought about what other skills he had that would be useful in the art world. At the time, he worked at a gallery in Pioneer Square and loved the job, so he decided to open a gallery himself in 1983.

During the first months of their relationship, Larry lived in a ground-floor apartment and was doing framing there at Greg's encouragement. Often Greg would come by at night and tap on the window or find it conveniently open. Later that year, Greg encouraged him to open his own frame shop. The support the two gave each other during their early years as business owners brought them together, and thoughts of that time in the '80s still fill them with affection and gratitude after many years of professional success. Larry's shop, Gallery Frames, is widely known for good craftsmanship and personal customer service, and the Greg Kucera Gallery is an established, yet provocative, staple in the Seattle arts community.

"We couldn't get married at the time," Larry said, "but being asked to move in with someone was like a proposal." Everyone close to them knew what it meant. Greg and Larry soon bought a house near Seattle's Volunteer Park—their first real home together. They found a house with a high-ceilinged basement to accommodate Larry's framing equipment, and remodeled the whole house to suit their tastes. Greg and Larry admit they are incredibly different from each other—the way they behave socially, their choices of clothing, their preferred foods, and even their walking speeds are entirely different—yet they have remodeled three houses together and started three businesses with hardly any disagreement.

They moved to Queen Anne in 1989 but found the neighborhood to be too quiet for their tastes so began plotting to reclaim their Volunteer Park house. Luckily it went on the market again in 1996, and they moved back in to find it more or less as they'd left it. They didn't think they'd find a more appealing home until a condo with a rooftop garden on Capitol Hill presented itself. Once again, they remodeled the interior themselves. "We used a tape measure and graph paper" was Larry's simple description of their technique. They filled the courtyard with their favorite flowers and their new home with their continuously growing art collection. "The gardens look great in early June but are probably at their best in mid-May, when the rhodies and azaleas are in full bloom," said Greg of the garden, which he outfitted with galvanized livestock watering tubs as planters.

Considering the two frequently comment on how different they are, it's remarkable how much common ground they have aesthetically. It helps that they are necessarily informed and well connected in the arts community because of the gallery, which has been an institution in

Pioneer Square for decades. Greg and Larry bought most of their art with no specific space in mind, but when they saw the rooftop condo, it was immediately apparent where certain things would go.

As their collecting progressed, every space became very valuable. "The Cris Bruch work that looks like a horn attached from the ceiling was bought because we felt we were running out of wall space," said Greg. "Likewise, we have two works that are corner related because we still have corners that are free but the wall space is getting more and more full."

Greg and Larry had been together for thirty years when Referendum 74 passed. They were sitting at home, watching as the votes were counted on TV, when their own conversation about marriage began. They'd hoped to marry for a very long time, but now that it was possible, they felt they needed to revisit the idea and discuss it to be sure it was what they really wanted. "We recognize this thirty-year relationship capped by a wedding seemed desultory rather than adventurous," said Greg. Over the next two days, an initially casual conversation became deeply emotional as they examined their reasons for being together. It was less like a proposal than a detailed affirmation of the love they'd known was true when they first decided to move in together.

Their friends, as well as their families, had long awaited the news. Despite the fact that when Larry was nineteen, his dad informed the Mormon church officials that Larry was gay, resulting in Larry's excommunication from the Mormon church. When two church officials showed up at his door, Larry introduced them to his boyfriend. He didn't bother to attend his trial. Having recently discovered the delights of Capitol Hill (a historically gay Seattle neighborhood) in the '70s, he was not exactly devastated by the loss. As fearful and reactionary as Larry's parents were when they discovered Larry was gay, the family has loved Greg almost as long as the two have been together. "They got over themselves. It only took them a few months," said Larry.

Greg and Larry spent about half a year planning the wedding. They considered having it at their cabin in Index, Washington, but it would have been much harder for the guests to get to, and their rooftop garden in town was too perfect for the occasion. One of Greg's high school friends, Cass Vaivadas, baked a red-and-black plaid raspberry cake to match Greg's jacket and cufflinks. Greg has an impressive collection of plaid clothing, particularly buffalo plaid, the red-and-black plaid (though buffalo are not known to favor the pattern as much as gay bears seem to). By far the element of the wedding that Greg and Larry put the most thought into was the ceremony itself. They invited Janice Niemi, a retired superior court judge and fellow art collector, to be their officiant, and they carefully composed their vows over a period of months.

Greg and Larry's hilarious wedding invitation included a list of things that would not be present at the ceremony: extravagant veils, children strewing endangered species of orchid petals, cakes shaped like buttocks, Irish setters as groomsmen, wedding rings, nipple rings, and miles of lace carried by trained kittens. Greg's and Larry's families were present, along with thirty years' worth of mutual friends, so many of whom were local artists and collectors that one guest commented, "If a bomb drops on us right now, the Seattle art scene is screwed."

Art critic Jen Graves gave an impromptu tour of their collection: the guest bedroom wallpapered with nineteenth-century *Shunga* (Japanese erotic art), the master closet containing a Grant Wood nude that was once confiscated as pornography, an original Tom of Finland drawing in the bathroom. In the garden, guests talked and sipped champagne among tubs overflowing with flowers, which were at their summer peak (and which, the two admit, they had a gardener fluff up for the occasion).

As the sun began to set, everyone gathered in the garden to hear the couple read the vows they had written. "As different as we are from each other, we so often see eye to eye," said Larry, "and we each feel we're the luckier one." "We wed now, among friends and family, without wedding rings or a church full of promises but with honor and truth, and belief in each other. . . . You are my mate to marvel at, and you are my mystery to unravel. After thirty years together, I am ever more grateful for you. It's simple: I loved you then; I love you now. I will have you and hold you, until death alone may part us," Greg's vows concluded. There were tears and applause that some of those in attendance had been hoping to give for decades, and then the two young men who Greg said they'd "borrowed from Saint Mark's" sang a beautiful version of Greg and Larry's song, "Make Our Garden Grow" from *Candide*. The plaid cake was served in the newlyweds' living room beside a ten-foot-tall sculpture of a pencil. At most weddings, there is some representation of the life a couple will have together that guests are invited to share and celebrate, but it's rare to know what that life will actually be like. A wedding like a party with a symbolic piñata that's contents are yet unknown. With their piñata already long-dropped, Greg and Larry's legal marriage should have been an anniversary party, yet there was something uniquely beautiful about a wedding held in an enduringly happy home, a celebration as carefully cultivated as their love.

# DECORATIONS

## Katherine & Kathleen

WHILE THERE WERE NO BEER BONGS, overturned cars, or unexplained corpses at the party in Seattle one night in 2013, Katherine behaved as if she were on spring break because she was. She was visiting from Alabama, where she was in grad school. This was the night she met Kathleen, who was at least attempting to have a more subdued evening. "She hated me the first time we met," Katherine said of that night. The following morning, she came to a garden party at Kathleen's (the kind with more actual dirt and pruning implements than mimosas). "In walks this girl who looks really good, and not annoying as all hell," Kathleen recalled. She was impressed that Katherine was actually wearing gardening pants—tight with a floral print. They made eggs and roasted-root-vegetable hash together. "Our first real encounter, her being a southern belle and all, she helped me perfect my terrible attempt at fried eggs," said Kathleen. "Anyway, at this party she saw my bedroom. She will tell you one of the first things she instantly fell for was the décor in my bedroom . . . and the terrible neon boxer briefs I was wearing under my seriously awful ripped garden jeans."

The details that drew Katherine and Kathleen to each other were the first indication of a shared appreciation for—and similar tastes in—decoration and aesthetics. Their appearances are nearly as similar as their names, but the contrast between their personalities is apparent immediately. They describe themselves as classic type A and type B personalities; when I met them, Katherine was writing thank-you cards to all of their wedding guests, while Kathleen volunteered stories and offered me a drink. Katherine is very driven and industrious, whereas Kathleen's great talent is with people.

Even before Kathleen ever met Katherine, she referred to her as "the wife." She briefly dated a woman she met on OkCupid who had *also* dated Katherine. In conversation with this woman, Kathleen jokingly referred to Katherine as "your wife in Alabama." Soon after the garden party where she met Kathleen, Katherine finished grad school and moved in with their mutual ex while looking for an apartment.

When Kathleen learned Katherine was back in Seattle, they went out for drinks and nachos. Intending to be funny, Kathleen said she would never have a girlfriend if she didn't learn to eat more neatly, and Katherine replied she would happily lick her fingers. Kathleen thought it was only a joke, but in the following weeks she began to wonder.

While Kathleen and Katherine's intentions during this time were ambiguous, they leaned enough toward something both of them recognized that they texted the mutual ex an apology. She responded with enough of a mixed message that things stayed as they were between Katherine and Kathleen, until they attended a funeral and a wedding together on the same day. They left the funeral, of a mutual friend who was shot by the police, and drove to a wedding in Poulsbo, Washington, where they would have their own wedding sooner than either of them could have guessed. Katherine became so anxious she hit a car when she pulled into the parking lot. Afterward, they went to Kathleen's house. They both felt overwhelmed and confused—the day's combination of events seemed like some terrible joke—but they found talking about it made its more frightening elements easier to deal with. Neither of them wanted to part. For the first time, they stayed the night together.

Many nights together were to follow. They talked about everything, eager to know each other's histories. Kathleen grew up on the Tulalip Indian Reservation in Washington. Her dad is Norwegian and her mom is Anishinabe. "My family was all about human connection," said Kathleen. "My mom used to say, when you die, it doesn't matter how successful you were; it matters how many people show up to your funeral." In seventh grade she moved to Sultan, Washington, with her family. The transition from reservation life was distracting in a variety of ways. She didn't realize she liked women until she went to Cornish College of the Arts (a theme in this book, it seems) for music. "I thought I didn't like boys because I liked activities," she said with a grin.

Katherine's parents in Dallas put great emphasis on professional and academic success, and Katherine achieved it—she went to the University of Washington two years early for a degree in political science. She moved to Portland for a year, where, she said, cryptically, "things got weird," before moving to Alabama for her MBA.

After Kathleen and Katherine's discovery that funerals were better in each other's company came the discovery that sitting around the house doing nothing together was better as well. They spent most nights together. They gardened and had a weekly date at a Caribbean restaurant called Rumba. On weekends, they went to artists' showcases and boutiques—anywhere they could be in the proximity of beautiful and well-made objects. "One of the first gifts I bought Katherine was a refinished vintage Victorian side table from a random boutique," Kathleen recalled.

They'd been dating a few months when by chance Kathleen found she had to be out of her house on the same day Katherine was moving into a new place. Kathleen had resolved not to move in with anyone she wasn't going to marry. Their decision to move in together was an implicit proposal they were both aware of but initially too nervous to talk about. "Then one night we were lying on the couch," said Kathleen. "I said, are we engaged? What's going on?

She said, yeah, I think we're engaged." There was a moment of silence and then adrenaline, a mixture of fear and joy.

Kathleen was afraid to tell her grandma she was with a woman, but ultimately the only thing that upset her grandma was that she found out on Facebook. That winter she even bought Katherine a Christmas present.

Both women's families had been completely blindsided when they came out, and Katherine's family had some reservations about the wedding—after all, they had only been dating a year. Having never met Kathleen, they worried the engagement was some wild byproduct of grad school, like a regrettable tattoo. Kathleen's dad joked about it in a way she didn't find very funny, saying it was his fault she was marrying a woman because he told her she couldn't date a man before she was thirty. He still jokes about it, but the tone of the jokes is loving. He treats Katherine as his own daughter.

Katherine and Kathleen wanted a vintage-inspired, time-traveling gay wedding—as Kathleen put it, "We wanted our wedding to feel like it was fifty years prior. To seem classic. Something that should have been happening a hundred years ago that wasn't, and now is. We wanted our grandparents and parents—all of our guests, really—to be awed by the beauty, to be taken back in time to a place of nostalgia and to see how normal, loving, and beautiful this wedding was. Two women, in love, committing to a life together, as humans have for centuries. Beautiful. Simple. Vintage."

Fortunately, their grandparents were happy to help—their grandmas sent doilies and lace as decorations, and Kathleen's grandma Marie helped the two make 120 jars of strawberry-rhubarb jam.

Kathleen describes her family as collectors of people, and they're clearly prepared to accommodate the ever-growing collection—her dad, a welder, built twelve ten-foot farm tables, a bar cart, and tractor-seat chairs from scrap metal and wood for the wedding. The furniture turned out even more beautiful than the exorbitantly expensive rentable tables that inspired it, but it was a tremendous amount of work.

She and Katherine began combing Goodwills, estate sales, and Craigslist for decorations. They picked up eighteen chairs from two different estate sales in the pouring rain and stopped on Whidbey Island late one night to pick up a vintage desk. They actually bought a truck to transport decorations to Poulsbo where the wedding was held at the beach house of a family Kathleen used to nanny for. During the weekends preceding the wedding, Katherine had occasion to wear her stylish gardening pants as she and Kathleen gardened at the beach house.

Rumba, where they'd had their weekly date night since they first started seeing each other, agreed to cook for the wedding, though they don't normally do catering.

Nearly everything for the wedding that wasn't made by Katherine and Kathleen or family members was something

the couple found while on dates or simply driving around together. This included the bartender, whom they found in Poulsbo. It was her first day bartending. They overheard her talking to another customer, thought she was hilarious, and invited her to bartend at their wedding. By the time they were married, preparation for their wedding had lasted a third of their relationship.

Though it hailed twice the morning of the wedding (freakish because it was August 2), by the time guests arrived, the weather was beautiful. Katherine's family flew in from Alabama, Oklahoma, and Texas. Kathleen's friends from Cornish played folk music while their families, including all the family members they'd "collected," ate tacos and played lawn games under a banner that read "Mrs. and Mrs." At the end of the afternoon, everyone gathered around to watch Kathleen and Katherine's traditional Native American blanket ceremony, in which the mothers of the brides, having blessed the couple, cover them with a blanket to symbolize the beginning of their new life together. The newlyweds were exhausted, having made, gathered, and organized so many elements of the wedding themselves, but to see all these pieces that each had a story come together just as they'd hoped was incredibly satisfying. They time-traveled exactly as people should, taking all their favorite things and everyone they love with them.

# INVITES AND FAVORS

## Hannah & Molly

AFTER A SOUTHERN-STYLE VALENTINE'S brunch in New York, Hannah found herself alone in the kitchen doing dishes. However, she was soon joined in the kitchen by Molly. They discovered they'd known of each other for some time—Hannah's roommate, who was also Molly's best friend from college, had told both of them she knew another lesbian who worked in publishing. Hannah was working for Ballantine Books, part of Random House, and Molly worked for Cash Money Content (part of Cash Money Records), which primarily publishes a genre called "urban lit"—best-selling titles include *Justify My Thug* and *Payback Ain't Enough*. The party was enjoyable: they ate biscuits and bacon, drank bourbon lemonade, and invented a game in which an excerpt of a trashy romance novel was read aloud and everyone went around the table writing an ending. It was the Apples to Apples of smut. But the best part, they agreed, was doing dishes and

chatting afterward. They had rarely enjoyed doing dishes as much as they did at that party.

Hannah could have taken the same train home, but she liked Molly so much she decided to part ways at the door— she was in a relationship, though one she knew was on its way out. Before leaving they promised to have a "business lunch" soon to chat about publishing. Molly was similarly trying to extricate herself from a bad relationship. She had recently moved in with a woman from Japan, despite the fact that Molly knew no Japanese and the other woman knew very little English. That they were living together, in fact, was the result of a miscommunication.

Two months later, they were both single and met up for the promised "business lunch," which led to a series of what they called "non-date dates." Molly was determined to stay single for a while—she wanted to see Hannah, but she also wanted to have a "summer of Molly." She asked her brother what to do. "I'm not ready to date my wife yet," she said of Hannah. "You can date both," he told her, but added, "You need to go find the angel on your shoulder, because I'm the devil." So she went out on an impromptu date with a woman from Argentina. They went to a stand-up show, which the woman ruined by talking all the way through. Molly left thinking of Hannah and the jokes she'd missed.

Soon afterward, on another non-date date at a Ukrainian restaurant in the East Village, they had another conversation so engaging that neither of them wanted to leave. When she got home that night, Hannah told her roommate, their mutual friend, that she'd met her future wife. Molly told her sister that the non-date had been the best date of her life.

They went on several more non-dates in Chinatown, where Molly lived. One night in the summer, they played squash beneath the Manhattan Bridge and later sat squeezed into a single lawn chair on Molly's roof drinking Simpler Times beer into the evening. Hannah wanted to tell Molly how she felt about her—she knew she would, but she had no idea how Molly would react. Finally, when the sun had gone down and what on previous occasions would have been the time to go home was approaching, Hannah said, "I won't let you be my non-girlfriend forever." To her joy and relief, Molly confessed she'd been feeling the same way.

Hannah grew up in Ohio and California. She had always loved to read, and after college at Oberlin, she spent a couple of years doing odd jobs and making her way into the publishing industry. Molly's way into the publishing industry was perhaps even more winding. She also grew up in Ohio, where her mom ran a children's bookstore and her dad owned a small company that made a butter-and-olive-oil spread called Olive-It. As a kid, Molly used to go to Whole Foods with her dad to promote the spread, dressed as a cow stuffed inside an olive like a pimento. She went to the University of Wisconsin–Madison for international studies, then worked in Kenya, Florence, and Korea, as a social worker, professor's assistant, and elementary school English teacher, respectively, and eventually landed at a literary agency in New York.

After the transition from non-girlfriends to regular girlfriends, Molly and Hannah quickly tired of going across town to get to each other's apartments. "There were many mornings when she went scrounging in my closet for something to wear to work. Thank God we're both women," said Molly. A little less than a year later, they moved in together.

"We U-Hauled it a bit," admitted Hannah. It was becoming clear the things they'd told their friends and family about future wives weren't exaggerations or idle comments. Travel-loving Molly began to fantasize about the ideal place to propose.

Through Airbnb, Molly reserved a cabin outfitted with a gorgeous kitchen and an outdoor grill on a beach in Tulum, Mexico. Rather than pick out a ring to propose with, since she knew Hannah would want to pick rings out together, Molly decided to do something more out of the box. Since their favorite thing to do together is cook and they were going to Mexico, Molly decided to have a stainless-steel fish grill basket engraved with their middle names, Byron and Iris. She planned to propose on the beach while they grilled freshly caught fish together. Unfortunately, the Airbnb spot fell through the week before they left for Mexico.

Molly scrambled to book the only other place available over Christmas vacation. It had no grill, no kitchen, and no bathroom.

After searching in vain for any cheap authentic Mexican food their first night in Tulum, they ended up eating at a fancy restaurant across the street from their new accommodations. "It was like we hadn't left Brooklyn," said Molly. "Pistachio-crusted everything." They woke up the following morning with the worst food poisoning either of them had ever experienced. They were so feverish they were hallucinating and could hardly stand up. Molly actually wondered if they had malaria. The new Airbnb shack was now the last place they wanted to be. "I was sweating in this thatched hut with scorpions falling out of the ceiling," said Hannah.

Obviously, Molly wanted to hold off on the proposal until they were no longer throwing up and surrounded by bugs. She couldn't find any fish to grill anyway, and she had learned that beach fires were illegal at the new hut. When they could walk again, they went on to Mérida, a town Molly's parents had visited before they were married. Her dad had bought so many hammocks there that he couldn't afford the trip back.

On the last day of the trip, they were still feeling a little gross, but they had an exceptionally good time. The moment felt right to Molly, though it wasn't exactly as she'd imagined. She pulled out the grill basket. "It was wrapped in garbage bags, and looked like a tennis racket," said Hannah. "I thought, I don't want to play tennis, I feel terrible." When she realized what it really was, she felt joy. "I said yes, of course," she said with a grin. "I somehow didn't question being proposed to with a grill basket."

Molly is very close with her family—they knew about the engagement grill basket before it was commissioned. "She talks to her mom and sister nearly every day," said Hannah. Molly had lived all over the world for years and began to really miss being near them. Her sister lives near Seattle with her family, and her mom and dad recently moved to Whidbey Island, just outside Seattle. Molly and Hannah loved living in New York, but when Molly's dad got sick, they knew they were too far away. Hannah agreed to give living in Seattle a try. Molly could do her job remotely, but Hannah had to find new work. Molly was blown away by Hannah's willingness to transplant her life—it was one of those gestures that reinforces every sweet thing a person has said.

Planning for the wedding began before the move. They envisioned a sort of wedding tour, traveling everywhere to visit all the people they loved to celebrate with them, but Molly's parents' house on Whidbey Island enticed them with its beauty and convenience. Molly's parents, who had heard about Hannah since their first non-date, were thrilled to host the wedding. Molly's sister found their wedding dresses and flowers. Hannah's parents were equally excited, though learning that she was dating Molly had been the first they'd heard of her preference for women. They are divorced, but both told her the same thing: they just want her to be happy.

Hannah and Molly decided to have a very small wedding, so they decided to send "Don't Save the Date" cards and a small favor to all the people they would have visited on their wedding tour or invited to a large wedding. On her first trip to Mexico as a teenager and later in Kenya, Molly had collected tin enamel mugs and plates, so she came up with the idea of tin mugs as a favor. Hannah had also used a set of tin enamelware as camping dishes on trips in her childhood and loved the idea. They thought a camp mug would be fitting for their outdoorsy new home; after years of living a city life, they were delighted to be surrounded by so much nature and found themselves outdoors kayaking, canoeing, or hiking nearly every weekend. To personalize the mugs, Molly designed a logo for the two of them, and her sister, an art conservator, taught her to emboss the logo onto the enamel mugs.

The "Don't Save the Date" note they sent with the mugs read:

Dear family and friends, as you already know, we're getting married! We'll be having a small ceremony with immediate family on Whidbey Island in Washington on September 20th, then we'll be heading to Kauai, Hawaii, for our honeymoon. If we were having a big wedding you'd obviously be invited and we'd give you party favors and it would be a night you'd never forget. In lieu of this fabulous night, here is the party favor: a camping mug, in homage to our new outdoorsy Pacific Northwest lives. Love you all! Ciao for now!

Molly carved several stamps—a coat of arms with an *M* and an *H* for the mugs, and images of various symbols of their relationship on the "Don't Save the Date" notes. The back of the notes read, "A Pictorial History of Byron and Iris" amid a pork bun from Chinatown; a can of Simpler Times from the night Hannah told Molly how she felt about her; a conch empanada from a trip to Puerto Rico; and Mount Rainier, which is just outside their new hometown. A jaunty pineapple represented their upcoming honeymoon in Kauai.

The wedding was just what Hannah and Molly had hoped—a low-stress gathering of close family. They ate and drank memorably; after having a short ceremony on the beach, the newlyweds and their eleven guests made their way to a small local restaurant on Whidbey Island called the Oystercatcher for a nine-course lunch. They spent the rest of the wedding weekend boating and clamming. Whidbey Island in September alternates between crystalline sunshine and fog, and they were incredibly lucky to enjoy the last true weekend of summer. Hannah and Molly both felt deeply content. "The most important thing in a relationship is to feel comfortable around each other and enjoy talking about anything together," said Hannah. "That's what you'll be doing for the rest of your days: just talking about bullshit. I've never felt happier just talking about nothing than I do with Molly."

# PART III

# Ceremony

# WEDDING COUTURE

## Kitten & Lou

KITTEN LARUE AND LOU HENRY HOOVER had performed together in several stage shows over the course of two years before they ever had a one-on-one conversation. To this day, neither of them knows why. It's particularly odd considering they had a mutual best friend, drag performer BenDeLaCreme. After a performance at a Seattle club called the Triple Door, the three finally spent an evening together. "I like Kitten," Lou told Ben afterwards. "Yeah, I do too!" Ben replied. "No," said Lou, "I like her in a different way than you do." Soon afterward, Kitten invited Lou to join her burlesque troupe, the Atomic Bombshells.

Kitten and Lou both laughed when asked about their first date, which consisted of drunkenly hooking up under a table during a drag show involving a Beyoncé impersonator. "Lou's classy first line was, 'Are we going to make out or what?'" Kitten said. Thus began what they call their summer "showmance." Putting on a show in Provincetown,

Massachusetts, was difficult because of the sheer number of competing acts. Many clubs book two or three acts a night. "You have to go out in the streets in drag and convince people to see your show," Kitten said.

Though Kitten and Lou were working hard, everything felt like fantasy that summer; they spent most of their time in costume, partied every night, and, for a few precious days at the end of the trip, had an apartment to themselves. Sequins and tulle abounded. Their romance felt unreal, like something from a movie, even when after two weeks, Lou wrote Kitten a very serious love letter. Kitten still remembers when Lou mentioned that it made her sad that their summer romance wasn't ending in "two wedding dresses."

The reality of their feelings crashed in on them at the end of the summer, when the prospect of not seeing each other anymore sent them both into a stomach-dropping, sweaty panic. For various reasons, Kitten couldn't give Lou the attention she was hoping for right away, but to prove she was serious, she gave Lou her sorority ring and a mix tape. BenDeLaCreme, who heard the tape on endless repeat because he and Lou lived together, described it as "the most romantic mix tape anyone has given anyone ever."

The relationship took off quickly after Provincetown. Kitten and Lou dated for a year without performing or touring before a month-long trip to New Orleans, where they made their first duet acts, including a wedding-themed act that Lou proposed. In New Orleans, they had the opportunity to try living together for real while subletting an apartment during their show. They loved it, both of them nervous and giddy that their act together involved a faux wedding.

Lou got up one morning and knew she was going to propose for real when the right moment arose. She's a world-class planner, as evidenced by her carefully conceived shows, but this time she decided it would be more romantic if her proposal were spontaneous. The two went for a walk in the park, where Lou planned to propose if Kitten sat down on a bench. She never did, and Lou became increasingly nervous. "She was acting like such a weirdo," said Kitten. They had dinner together in a nice restaurant, which seemed like an ideal place, but Kitten complained about the noise of the generator there and then the music. Finally, on a bike ride to a drag show that evening, Lou announced they were pulling over. She dropped her bike to the ground and got down on one knee. Kitten said yes without hesitation. They held each other, oblivious to passing cars and everything else in the universe until they were interrupted by a man yelling "Hey! You guys got a sandwich? I don't want money, just gimme a sandwich!" They simultaneously noticed the sandwich-demander's Provincetown sweatshirt. It was as if he were there to bless the wedding.

Lou grew up in Massachusetts, went to Michigan to study dance, and then moved to Seattle to work with modern-dance choreographer KT Niehoff. Her parents are fairly conservative, but after they'd had some time to process the fact that Lou liked women, they were loving and supportive. Their attitude toward marriage equality is paradoxical. Their politics would indicate that they probably voted against gay marriage, yet they financed much of Kitten and Lou's wedding—Lou's father even danced her down the aisle.

Kitten's mom and stepfather were more difficult. She is in contact with her mother—she occasionally texts small talk and soup recipes—but Kitten's parents did not attend the wedding or even acknowledge it. Kitten grew up in Louisiana, studied English literature and art history at the University of Southern Mississippi, then, as she puts it, "moved to New Orleans first, where I started burlesque, and then to Seattle." Her mom and stepdad, who basically raised her, were into crystals and Indian gurus when she was a kid, but then when she was a teenager, one conversation with a preacher turned them into Christian religious fanatics. They were suffering financial hardship at the time, and were picking up their co-op order from the church. Perhaps the conversation with the preacher affected them so strongly because they were caught at a vulnerable moment. It's hard to say—whatever their beliefs, they had always gone to extremes with certain things. They now belong to an obscure proto-Christian sect that doesn't celebrate

Christmas because of the holiday's pagan origins. Lou sent them a letter before the wedding, explaining how much some acknowledgment of the event would mean to Kitten and herself, and requesting an addition to a crucial part of Kitten's wedding outfit, a broach bouquet full of little gifts from loved ones, but never heard back. Kitten and Lou's disappointment was visible when they recalled the silence of Kitten's mother and stepdad. Correspondence since the wedding has been sporadic small talk via text, and the marriage is still ignored. Fortunately, Kitten's biological dad was delighted to come to the wedding, and walked her down the aisle. They had a wonderful time together.

The broach-bouquet debacle was the only real trouble the two had with their wedding outfits, which were designed by their longtime costumer, Danial Webster, who specializes in costumes for drag and burlesque. Lou and Kitten wanted a matching suit and dress, and they wanted them to be outrageous—something fitting for the celebration of a relationship that began onstage. They chose a classic Tiffany-blue fabric with hand-painted gold leopard print as a material. Having matching outfits made was nothing out of the ordinary for the couple; they almost always perform in matching outfits, and frequently match offstage as well. "We have matching leopard-print Betsey Johnson backpacks," said Kitten. "It's a bit of an issue."

Lou was excited to have an impeccably fitted suit. There was no talk of two wedding dresses, even though that was Lou's metaphor for staying together in her first showmance love letter. In a sense, both of their outfits were drag, but dapper Lou said, "It felt like how I'd present myself in my actual life." Lou very rarely wears dresses onstage, performing almost exclusively as a drag king, though she occasionally does what the two describe as "faux queen drag." Danial Webster told her making a suit for her slender frame was like sewing doll clothes.

Kitten's wedding dress was highly customized—she was actually able to choose the size of her bust and where her waist would be. She, too, felt there was an element of drag to the outfit—its flashiness, its exaggeration and grandiosity—but also that it was also an accurate representation of her identity. Kitten's sartorial philosophy: "More is more. The higher the hair the closer to God. Life's too short to wear khaki shorts." Kitten hardly ever plays masculine roles onstage (one notable occasion was her performance as an older version of Lou as a grandpa) but says that she brings a certain butch swagger to her high-femme persona. "As queer people, we kind of get to reinvent the wheel," she said. "We have more freedom than the typical straight couple to make marriage whatever we want. People already think it's weird we're getting married." In truth, there is an element of drag to most wedding clothing, in the sense that it's designed to accentuate and exaggerate traditionally gender-specific characteristics. The idea of a gender spectrum is so new that often the "presentation" part of gender presentation is taken for granted or ignored.

Kitten and Lou took about five months to plan their wedding, with BenDeLaCreme as artistic director, but much like their shows, it all came together at the last moment. This was partly because Ben had to leave town to film the reality show *RuPaul's Drag Race* midway through the wedding preparation and didn't return until four days before the ceremony. "He was out on his lawn at six a.m., spray-painting two hundred ceramic cats," said Kitten. Ben also spray-painted hundreds of roses blue—Kitten and Lou wanted blue roses, but the cost of dyed flowers was prohibitive. On top of the last-minute decorating, their outfits weren't entirely finished until the morning of the wedding. The two thought they would be more relaxed than most on their wedding day, since to some degree weddings are like performances, but they couldn't brace themselves for the overwhelming, drug-like mixture of anxiety and joy unique to weddings.

Nevertheless, as their invitation promised, the wedding was truly an "extravaganza of eleganza" that went off without a hitch. Their venue of choice, the Georgetown Stables, was bedazzled with plastic clowns, ceramic cats, balloons of all sizes, a silver fountain of ice water, and pyramids of multicolored miniature cupcakes. Every guest had decorated themselves for the event just as impressively. It was practically raining silk and rhinestones. Bubbles pouring out of a machine in the courtyard floated between the many piñatas in the trees. There was even a horse-shaped bouncy castle. The brides emerged in their matching cream-and-blue leopard-print ensembles, accompanied by beaming parents. The ceremony was officiated by performer Waxie Moon, who announced he was "Reverend Moon" for the evening. When the couple kissed, their groomsmen and bridesmaids popped two enormous golden balloons, showering the assembly with white crepe paper, and everyone cried. It was a glamorous wedding, yet nothing seemed superfluous. It was, like their suit and gown, perfectly tailored. Its element of drag was true to life—or at least to the part of life in which the outrageous fantasy of love is realized.

# RELIGION

## Britton & Kurt

"O PALINURUS, TOO TRUSTFUL OF THE sky and sea, you will lie naked on an unknown shore," read the lines Kurt quoted from *The Aeneid* in his first e-mail to Britton. Britton couldn't believe it. He had translated *The Aeneid* as a Latin minor in college but had been most captivated by the passage this line was from—so captivated that he'd taken the name Palinurus as part of his e-mail address. He hardly paid attention to his messages from dating sites anymore, having gone on hundreds of first-and-last dates that left him feeling nothing. He had been single almost fourteen years.

Kurt was impressed that Britton recognized the passage and also by the pictures on his profile. "He had legs to die for!" Kurt said with a grin. They had a two-month-long e-mail correspondence, largely about their hopes for relationships. It was the careful conversation of people who had loved and been hurt. "The interesting thing is we negotiated all the terms of our relationship before we even met," said Britton.

It was nerve-racking for both of them when they finally met in person, at a Hawaiian restaurant in Seattle. What if their profile pictures were not an accurate representation of reality? What if they annoyed each other? Fortunately, they both thought each other even better looking in person than in pictures, and even more charming in person than in print. "Once I met Kurt I realized he was good down to the core," said Britton. "I knew he was the real deal." Britton was flying to Italy the next day, and Kurt offered to drive him to the airport at four in the morning. Britton thought it was just a polite offer but was amazed to actually see him on his doorstep before dawn.

One evening, on the way home from an exotic-reptile fair, Kurt asked Britton, "Can I say I love you?" Britton, who had been hurt by frivolous use of that word in the past, said no. A week later, before traveling to Napa Valley, Kurt asked if he could call Britton his boyfriend. Again, Britton declined. Kurt came back to Seattle with a gift of two extremely expensive bottles of wine. "I was shocked. He was very hurt when he left," said Britton. The following month, Britton heard a knock on his door one night, and it was Kurt, who said that he didn't care if they said they loved each other or if they were boyfriends but that he had to sleep in the same bed with Britton. Britton decided he was comfortable with that. In the middle of the night, Kurt began having a nightmare. He sat up in bed and said, "Damn it, Britton. I don't care—I love you!" Britton told him that it was okay and that he loved him too. The next time they went out, Kurt seemed upset. Finally, in the car, he asked Britton why they couldn't say they love each other. He had been completely asleep during his nighttime conversation with Britton and didn't remember a thing. When he finally heard Britton repeat their exchange, he was overwhelmed with joy and relief. Conversation on their next date was more pleasant and was held entirely while both of them were conscious.

As Kurt and Britton got to know each other, they discovered they had several unlikely connections. The reason Kurt could quote Virgil was that he had studied Latin for four years in seminary—he was a former Catholic priest. As a child in Tacoma, Washington, he went to Catholic elementary school, and then at thirteen, he was invited to enroll in the seminary, which proved to be a needed escape from his turbulent home life. He was a highly capable student, but he believes the priests and nuns of his home parish in Tacoma, aware of the abuse and addiction in his family, decided that life at Saint Edward Seminary would remove him from a severely declining home environment and provide the structure he so sorely needed. The year after Kurt graduated from Saint Edward, both of his parents died of alcoholism.

School and the church, as always, were a refuge. He excelled in his graduate theology program and was ordained as a priest in 1978. He wanted to share the aspects of his faith that had helped him weather a difficult youth, and he succeeded—people still write to tell him how he helped them during his years as a priest.

Kurt had always known he was gay. At the time he joined the priesthood, he saw no inherent conflict between his sexuality and his religion, but when he'd been a priest for about ten years, the Vatican issued an official message that homosexuals were intrinsically disordered and that their having sex together was a "mortal sin." "I went to Archbishop Hunthausen," said Kurt. "He protested nuclear arms in Bangor, allowed gay people into the cathedral. A great man. I told him I cannot pastorally share this with the people I serve; I do not believe it." The archbishop explained that the teaching was not "ex cathedra" or infallible and certainly wasn't the word of God. Archbishop Hunthausen suggested that Kurt take a year off and consider how he could maintain his vocation, but Kurt decided not to return to the priesthood. When the HIV epidemic reached Seattle, the new course of his life was clear to him. Thus began Kurt's work in disease care and prevention, starting at the Northwest AIDS Foundation (now the Lifelong AIDS Alliance).

Britton had a more difficult time finding a professional calling but was just as quick to act when he saw others suffering or being mistreated. He was born in Limestone, Maine, and grew up in Delaware. His father was in the air force and met his mother while stationed in Japan during the Korean War. Britton's parents were atheists, but his mother's beliefs were heavily influenced by Shinto. Britton was a math major in college and hated it. "I just did math because I wanted to prove I could do it," Britton explained. "All your life you're attracted to people of the same sex, and you're thinking, 'This feels so right, but everybody says it's wrong.' You make a lot of stupid mistakes doing things other people think you should do—in your career choices and everywhere else. I didn't begin to trust my instincts until I was fifty."

Several years after college, Britton went on to law school. His first year, some of the upperclassmen were harassing gay students and sent a list of "known and suspected lesbians" to professors. They also taped *Penthouse* centerfolds to the lockers of some of these students. Britton and some friends started a gay students' association to combat homophobia. He and another member traveled from class to class offering support for gay students, resulting in his ostracism at the school by nearly everyone outside the association.

It was around this time his life took an unexpected, perhaps counterintuitive turn. Every morning on his way to school, Britton walked by a Catholic church, which sometimes hosted lectures about Catholicism. "I had always wanted to learn how crazy these Catholics actually were," he said. "It was so weird to me that they thought the bread and wine were the actual body and blood of Christ." He decided to attend a lecture there. He was surprised to find that Catholic ideology resonated deeply with him.

"So much of it made perfect sense to me. I grew up with Japanese ideas about the role of the individual in society, which were echoed in the church," he said. By the time he moved to Seattle, he was a devout Catholic. An interesting coincidence: he moved partly out of admiration for Archbishop Hunthausen, whose diocese included Seattle.

As a priest who left the church and a man who was baptized in his thirties, Kurt and Britton have relationships with Catholicism that differ in the degree to which the men are able to reconcile Catholic ideology with their own. "The church has always taught through fear and guilt, not belief in oneself, one's connectedness to God," said Kurt. "I still believe in God. I think the problem is we believe we're separated from God's love. The kingdom is already here."

Perhaps because he came to the church as an adult, Britton views the church's regulations differently. "I think all these stupid rules are designed to affirm one principle: the inherent sacredness of sexuality," he said. Since his marriage to a man is against the rules of the church, Britton no longer takes communion. "A lot of people tell me I could go to [a liberal] parish, take communion, and be exactly who I am," said Britton. "Maybe they're right, but I don't feel that's consonant with the vision of a universal church, and I need to honor that. I knew exactly what I was getting into. It's a huge sacrifice to me. Though what I have is utterly and completely worth it." "I probably have a special place in hell for influencing a convert," Kurt added, smiling wryly.

While they may have some disagreements about religion, spirituality is something the two bond over, and they're comfortable with the fact they access it in different ways.

Kurt and Britton had been together eleven years and shared two homes (one of which was haunted—a tale that deserves another entire chapter) when they became engaged. They'd discussed marriage when Referendum 74 passed, but Britton was still surprised when he arrived home from work late one night and Kurt dropped to one knee. They laugh when they tell the story of the proposal, how Britton's rush to put down an armload of groceries caused him to blurt out, "Yes, I know what you're asking and the answer's yes, of course yes" before Kurt, kneeling in front of him, even had a chance to get three words out.

Kurt and Britton chose the Chinese Room in Seattle's Smith Tower for their wedding. They were the first same-sex couple to marry in the historic tower, a popular wedding venue. Appropriately, the room was decorated with images of dragons—Britton's and Kurt's Chinese astrological signs, the rat and the dragon, respectively, are two of the most compatible in the zodiac. Long before he met Kurt, Britton got a dragon tattoo in hopes of attracting a dragon.

They asked their friend Jim to be their officiant. Jim is also a former priest, who left the church before Kurt did for similar reasons and later worked with Kurt in public health for years. Kurt and Britton's cat, Pyewacket, was as much help as anyone during preparation for the wedding. On advice from his friend Christine, Kurt practiced his "Why I Want to Marry Britton" statement by blurting out "Pyewacket!" whenever emotions started to get the better of him.

The day of the wedding, friends and family filled the Chinese Room to capacity. When they were priests, Jim was impressed with Kurt's wedding ritual and used parts of it in his own. Who would have thought that, after all these years, Jim would provide the ritual for Kurt's wedding? Kurt and Britton barely managed not to cry while exchanging vows. Kurt's words were punctuated by several "Pyewackets," but neither his nor Britton's eyes stayed dry through the whole ceremony. In addition to having a former Catholic priest as an officiant, they performed a Shinto wedding ceremony called *san-san-kudo*, in which the marrying couple take three sips from three successively larger cups of sake, representing the deepening of love with time and the difficulties they will endure together.

"And so, now, we celebrate the good fortune of the former priest and the convert," Jim read. "Having found their way to the answer to their lifelong quest for vocation, for purpose, their mission, home. Who could have known, years ago, that their spiritual quest, their longing for 'the truth that sets us free,' would lead them to each other?"

# OFFICIANTS

---

## Joseph & Gary

JOSEPH DIDN'T LIKE DOGS, BUT IN 1998, having posted an ad in the newspaper in hopes of expanding his interests, he agreed to a dog-walking date with a guy named Gary. The ad's headline was "Two Peas out of the Pod." Joseph wrote that it wasn't important to be with somebody exactly like him, as long as the man he was with wanted to share adventures. This sounded attractive to Gary, who could start a conversation with anybody and was always up for an adventure. As it turned out, Gary's dog was the first Joseph ever really liked, and Gary was just the sort of person Joseph was looking for. They arranged another date that day. "Joseph could have moved in with me at the third week," Gary said of those early days, but things progressed slowly and steadily between them. "There was never a lightning-striking moment. It was more like love has grown between us," Gary said.

Joseph grew up in Seattle. He studied Romance linguistics at the University of Washington and worked as a technical writer at Microsoft. Impressively, he came out in high school. "I had a lot of chutzpah," he said. "It was 1979."

Gary grew up outside Washington, DC, in Arlington, Virginia. After his parents died when he was a teenager, he lived with his brother and three friends. "I was the cook," he said. He went to a small college called St. Andrews in North Carolina, where he was an education major, and later became a sign language interpreter for the deaf. He made a valiant effort to date women in college and actually moved to Seattle with a girlfriend. He'd known for some time why things with his girlfriend weren't working—he went to a famous gay bar called Tugs (RIP) the very night they broke up. At the time, Gary lived in Queen Anne, the neighborhood where Joseph grew up, and often walked his dog around the track at Joseph's old high school. "The big joke was I was looking for Joseph," Gary said.

When Gary and Joseph talk about each other, they're quick to mention how different they are yet have much more to say about the things they love doing together. When they aren't traveling, they go to art shows and see experimental theater. "For me, it just goes back to seeing punk shows at the Showbox and little satellite happenings in various galleries and theaters, like the old On the Boards on Fourteenth. For Gary, it goes back to his hippie roots in college," said Joseph. Their travels are usually preceded by research about museums and performances near their destination. Among their favorites: fire ballet, which is exactly what it sounds like, at a place called the Crucible in Oakland, California, and an aerial performance by an Argentinian group called De La Guarda that they saw in London. Performers burst through a paper ceiling in the rafters of a warehouse and lifted audience members into the air with them. Once, Joseph surprised Gary with a trip to Djerba, an island in Tunisia, at the end of a trip to France. On a trip to Amsterdam, they followed locals to a vaudevillian performance in a field. Gary, beaming, was clearly still blown away. "Joseph is my personal travel agent," he said.

They soon discovered another thing they do well together is entertain. While they spoke modestly of their parties, the events sounded as if they often verged on theater themselves. For their millennial New Year's party, they set up a fireworks display in Joseph's front yard. The theme in 2001 (the year they moved in together, after five years of dating) was, of course, a space odyssey, with outer space–appropriate attire required. They've hosted glam-rock parties, go-go parties, and a faux prom. "There was Occupy Seward Park," said Joseph. (Seward Park is the neighborhood where they live.) "Some of our friends came as one-percenters. They revealed themselves as activists at midnight—put on hoodies and took over the stereo."

For two years, they had the pleasure of living next door to their longtime friends Ed and Stacy. Ed is a carpenter and amateur astronomer—a Renaissance man, as Joseph and Gary describe him. He built his own house on

Whidbey Island and his own telescope. "Our famous line is 'Ed can do it!'" said Gary. Over the years, Joseph and Gary have become close friends with Ed, Stacy, and their family.

Gary and Joseph had been together for seventeen years when gay marriage became legal in Washington. Their friend Julie was so excited when Referendum 74 passed that she threw a party where she served a wedding cake topped with two grooms. None of her gay friends were married yet, but she'd been urging Gary and Joseph to have a wedding since long before it was legal.

A few days later, Gary and Joseph were walking their dog Rosemary in the park, talking about the party. Gary said, "When are we getting married, Joseph? Someone has to ask the other!" They stopped in the field where they were walking, and each asked the other. Both, of course, said yes. "Rosemary wagged her tail in blessing!" Gary recalled. "We'd probably have done it years before if we could have."

Joseph and Gary often called Ed when their plumbing or practically anything else broke. One night, they called him up to ask him to be their officiant, but they decided it would be funny to pretend at first that their basement was flooding. They acted panicked. "Oh God, we don't know how to turn the water off!" Joseph told him. When his flustered plumbing questions began, they laughed. He was honored by the invitation to be their officiant and relieved he wasn't going to spend the evening wading through basement water.

"I'm not sure if he cried, but I think he was a bit overcome," said Gary. "We knew he could do it because Ed can do anything!" Ed took his role very seriously and talked to the men individually about what they planned to say to each other.

When Joseph's mother heard he was finally getting married, she gave Gary the diamond from her engagement ring, which they had set in a custom-made gold wedding band. Gary had hoped his brother Gordon would be his best man, since Gary had been Gordon's best man in 1973, when he was nineteen years old. Gordon, as eager to participate in the celebration as Joseph's mother, was happy to oblige. Several excited family members flew in from Virginia for the wedding. "My brother really stepped up for me at the wedding," said Gary. "It was a big deal for him to come to Seattle. They had a wonderful visit. We had great family time together."

Gary and Joseph's only wedding-planning disagreement was about the location. They'd already decided on the Lake Union Café and signed a contract when Joseph decided that since the wedding would be on May 5 (the anniversary of the day they met) a venue with an outdoor area would be preferable. Gary was annoyed, because Joseph had a history of thinking about things at length and then changing his mind. Fortunately, the same company owned another venue—the *Skansonia*, an antique ferry boat moored on Lake Union—which both of them liked. As soon as that decision was out of the way, they began planning the ceremony.

Joseph is often late—often enough that it was a running joke among the couple's friends. The couple's first idea was for Joseph to pull up to the ferry in a powerboat at the last moment and say, "Sorry I'm late!" Another was for Joseph to walk down the aisle with a female friend in a wedding dress. When they reached the altar, Gary would run up, grab Joseph, and yell, "Stop the wedding, he's mine! Now everyone sit down and enjoy the wedding. My wedding!"

The procession they decided on was inspired by the opening sequence from the classic glam-rock movie *Velvet Goldmine* and a fantasy Joseph had while on the treadmill at 24 Hour Fitness. Two little girls marched down the aisle with flowers, followed by a crowd of kids who ran all over the deck of the ferry waving streamers to Brian Eno's "Needle in the Camel's Eye."

The grooms appeared, accompanied by two mysterious figures in black spandex bodysuits—one with a multicolored cummerbund, and one with a pink tutu—who were twirling paper parasols. Under an arbor of white paper flowers made by Julie's daughter Grace, Joseph and Gary unwrapped the spandex-wearers to reveal their friends Jessica and Ed, who was looking sharp in gold aviators and a black suit. He said, "Well, you didn't expect a Martha Stewart wedding from Joseph and Gary, did you?" He gave a lovely speech about his long friendship with the couple. Everyone laughed when he described how they'd asked him to officiate. Both of them, particularly Gary, loved what he said after they exchanged vows: "I now pronounce you a legally married couple." Those were words neither of them thought he would ever hear. Many of the guests cried (myself included—I was fortunate enough to attend their wedding for my Wedding Crasher column), reminded of the love all the ceremony's theater was designed to celebrate and the charming personalities it reflected.

Joseph's mom stepped up to the arbor to give the marriage her blessing and read a (somewhat personalized) passage from the novel *Corelli's Mandolin*. "No, don't blush, I am telling you some truths. That is just being 'in love,' which any fool can do. Love itself is what is left over when being in love has burned away, and this is both art and a fortunate accident. Your father and I had it, we had roots that grew towards each other underground, and when all the pretty blossoms had fallen from our branches we found that we were one tree and not two." The passage had been Joseph's suggestion; when he read the book (a birthday gift from Ed) having been with Gary for over a decade, he couldn't believe how evocative it was of his own experience of love. He and Gary had no idea until a conversation they had with another pair of newlyweds in a hot tub in Costa Rica that it's frequently read at weddings. However, it's usually read in hopes of true love, but it had different significance for Joseph and Gary, who have long known they are one tree.

# IN-LAWS

## Kevin & Norbert

SOMEHOW, AT AN INTERNATIONAL CHORAL FESTIVAL attended by over six thousand people, Kevin, a member of the Seattle Men's Chorus, and Norbert, of Männerminne, a gay men's chorus from Berlin, Germany, noticed each other. The choral festival was an international event, with multiple choral groups, including Kevin's and Norbert's, on tour together. It was 1992, and Norbert had never been to the United States before. He made eye contact with Kevin across several crowded rooms before they finally spoke, the night before the tour left Seattle for Denver, both feeling an indefinite but irresistible pull. They slipped away from the festival one night and had dinner, and then spent the rest of their time in Denver together, until Norbert had to return to Germany. They were both surprised by how distressed they were at the prospect of leaving each other. "When we separated, it would have been easy to just say bye," said Kevin. "But we knew there was a hell of a lot going on. It wasn't just vacation." "There was no single event or realization that we loved each other; it was just like this immediate and strong unshakable awareness," Norbert added.

Norbert was in a relationship with someone back home—a fine relationship, but when he met Kevin, he knew immediately that he had found the most special person in his life. He felt compelled to tell the other man about Kevin as soon as he returned from the choral festival. His and Kevin's phone bills at the end of Norbert's first month home were nearly as expensive as a round-trip ticket from the United States to Germany.

Kevin had left New York just as the AIDS crisis struck, and its devastation terrified him to the point that, before he met Norbert, he had stopped dating for seven years. A man whom he had lived with for a decade, who started off as his boyfriend but became more like a brother, had recently died. "I had been careful, shut down, frightened," said Kevin. "Norbert's arrival poked at my heart enough to know I could open up again. We were so immediately comfortable with each other."

Norbert came to visit Kevin at Thanksgiving. When he returned to Germany, he missed Kevin so badly it woke him up at night. He lay awake and thought of him and the next time they would be together. Kevin visited Norbert's family in Germany for Christmas. He and Norbert stayed in several of Norbert's brothers' homes on the trip and were met with great hospitality. The drive to the village of Aldingen in a rented Ford Mondeo aggravated an old back injury from a car accident to the point where Kevin could barely walk. He was humiliated that he had to be helped out of the car like an old man upon his arrival, but Norbert's parents took care of him like one of their own kids.

Norbert's parents had lived as stateless refugees in France and moved to Germany, where the whole family was eventually naturalized, when Norbert was five. He grew up in a small town near the Black Forest and then moved to Heidelberg, where he got a master's in physics. The Berlin Wall still stood when he lived in West Berlin earning his doctorate. It was there that he began singing with the men's chorus.

Growing up in the Bronx in New York, Kevin dreamed of becoming a teacher. He got a scholarship to Mercy College, where he studied speech and language pathology, and afterward in 1978, he found his first teaching job, with young children who had communication disorders. "It was a dream job," he said. As if one dream job wasn't enough, he began doing some modeling on the side, which was what brought him to Seattle in 1981, where he'd found his first modeling gig, for a clothing company called Early Winters. An injury kept him in town longer than expected, and he made friends, found permanent work, and wound up staying. "My New York friends asked what the hell I was doing, but so many things had been handed to me—housing, jobs—I thought I'd leave when things feel crappy," said Kevin.

Eleven years later, the anticipated crappiness was nowhere to be found. Kevin bought a house and made many friends.

When he met Norbert, he was soon to be the father of his good friends' (a lesbian couple's) first child. "They basically adopted me," he said. When Norbert moved in with Kevin, it had been eighteen months since they met, but it felt as if they'd been waiting forever. The year after Norbert's arrival, Kevin had another baby with his friends. Their sons, now in college, were essentially raised by two moms and two dads.

There were many more happy trips to Germany. Norbert's mom, Elisabeth, actually learned English so that she could talk with Kevin. Norbert's dad, Bertl, reminded Kevin of his own father, who had died when Kevin was twenty-four—working class, thoughtful, astute, caring. "One of my highest moments in Bertl's company came at the airport as Norbert's parents departed after their first visit to Seattle," said Kevin. "He speaks no English except for the shared Deutsch and English words we teasingly exchanged—*gut*, pronto, *hallo*. But at the airport we embraced. He looked us each in the eye and said, in English, 'You are good men.' I still get choked up when I think of that moment. His approval of me, his son, our relationship, and our unfolding lives was profound. I would do anything for him. I had my dad anew."

Norbert spent quite a bit of time with Kevin's family as well and describes his relationship with them as "boringly and delightfully normal."

"I get along with his mother, Mary, most charmingly—we always have a good time when we get together. But we also talk honestly about health issues and all the other serious stuff one has to face as one gets older. I am struck by the very physical expression of affection in his family, down to his niece and nephew and their spouses and children. There are a lot of hugs."

For their tenth anniversary, in 2002, Norbert and Kevin went on a cruise to Alaska with Norbert's parents and Kevin's mother and sister. "Different worlds came together and coexisted beautifully," said Norbert. "My father was twelve years old when his family had to flee their home in what is now Serbia at the end of World War II, and he adopted some behaviors then that he carries with him to this day. It was very entertaining to watch the faces of my in-laws when, after they had finished their Caesar salads, he asked whether he could have their lemon wedges. They said yes; he proceeded to eat the lemons. 'It's good for you because they are rich in vitamins, you know.'"

Kevin and Norbert were vacationing in New York eleven years later when the Supreme Court's decision about gay marriage was rendered. Kevin asked a few people passing by to take pictures of him and Norbert in front of the street sign on the corner of Christopher and Gay Streets. After a few silly pictures, he announced, "Don't stop! I'm going to propose!" He knelt on the sidewalk and presented Norbert with a subway ring from the MTA museum with the logo of the subway line Kevin grew up near engraved on it, while their volunteer photographers cheered. "We were treated amazingly at ABC Kitchens, the restaurant we went to afterward," said Kevin. "I blurted out to the hostess we had just gotten engaged. The maître d' gave us free appetizers, free desserts, and a tour of the kitchen. A beautiful day!"

As it turned out, Kevin and Norbert had both been planning proposals for some time. A few days after Kevin proposed to Norbert, Norbert returned the gesture. On the southern tip of Roosevelt Island in New York City is a monument engraved with a quote from FDR's famous "Four Freedoms" speech. "That was where I proposed to Kevin," said Norbert. "I told him we should exercise our freedom to get married. My main reason for flying out to New York was to propose. I frankly expected the Supreme Court to decide otherwise." "It was really very equal, and fair, and sweet," Kevin said of the two proposals. Both of them felt lucky that they experienced the romance of receiving *and* making a proposal.

Kevin suggested they get married on Halloween, partly because the mixture of formal wedding attire and Halloween costumes would result in amazing photos. "I wanted the best, craziest Halloween party with a really moving ceremony in the middle," said Kevin.

Kevin's mother came from New York for the wedding, but Norbert's parents couldn't make it and were missed by everyone. "There was a lot of love and care," said Kevin of their families. "We have a rich history together. Norbert and I have lived in each other's family's homes so often." In ancient Jewish custom, the groom acquired his bride in exchange for a handkerchief to the bride's family. Kevin's mother is an excellent knitter, and Norbert's makes wonderful quilts, so they asked their moms to make them small fabric art pieces for the wedding to celebrate the coming together of their families.

On their wedding day, Kevin added the Halloween decorations he'd spent weeks gathering from thrift stores to Lake Union Café's antique décor, rumored to be left over from a speakeasy. The couple put together trick-or-treat bags as party favors, and signs on the bathroom doors read "hello boo-tiful" and "hello stud."

Norbert and Kevin invited a small number of close friends and family to watch them sign their documents and then welcomed the rest of their guests for a Kiddush (a traditional Jewish blessing recited over wine). To their delight, guests included Han Solo and the Gingerbread Man. In lieu of the traditional procession, they each chose a song to begin the ceremony. Kevin's was Michael Ball's "Love Changes Everything," which always makes him cry, thinking of how Norbert transformed his life. Norbert chose a

French chanson, "I Will Wait for You," in honor of those first nights in Germany alone after Kevin's visits when he lay awake thinking of him.

Their sons were MCs, and one of them kicked off the ceremony by addressing the guests: "You must be pretty frickin' excited to be invited to this, the social and wedding event of the season!" They had a champagne toast for Kevin and Norbert during the ceremony. Rather than traditional vows, Kevin and Norbert exchanged promises to each other, as well as the special fabrics made by their mothers. "We put the fabrics behind each other's backs, our families pressing us together as we embraced. It felt really symbolic, honoring of families, the taking in of a son," Kevin recalled. "The wedding was more about what we have built over the last twenty years than what the next decades hopefully will bring," said Norbert. Kevin spent nearly a month making a wedding album for Norbert's parents so that they would know how important they were at their son's wedding even though they were across the world. Kevin and Norbert keep their mothers' wedding fabrics in their living room as a daily reminder that when they found each other, they each found a new loving family as well.

**PART IV**

# Reception

# FOOD

---

## Chuck & Brian

BRIAN WAS NERVOUS THE NIGHT OF his first square dance. He'd ventured a few miles from Stanford, where he was in grad school, to attend a learn-to-dance night in Palo Alto, California, hosted by the El Camino Reelers, a gay and lesbian square dance club. He arrived a bit early, when few people were there, which as anyone who's been the first to a party knows does not help with shyness. Fortunately, the hospitality chair, Chuck, was setting up when he arrived, and was happy to make him a name badge and explain how the dance night would transpire. During the brief introduction, Chuck asked Brian for his first dance, and Brian agreed with a smile.

Newcomers filed in, and the room was soon a kaleidoscope of plaid. When the first dance began, Chuck and Brian took each other's hands and, in the tradition of the gender-neutral dance club, decided who would lead and who would follow. "As time goes on, dancers are given the opportunity to learn both follow and lead," Chuck said of the dance club. "After all, Ginger Rogers said she did everything Fred Astaire did, but backwards and in heels!"

Brian returned for weekly lessons, drawn partly by his growing friendship with Chuck, which had an element of yet-unspoken attraction. Autumn arrived, and Chuck began planning the annual Thanksgiving dinner he hosts for friends. Thanksgiving is Chuck's favorite holiday because it's a celebration of the people one chooses to be with and the gifts of life to be thankful for. This year, he invited Brian. Brian had a previous engagement, but was quick to suggest a date for leftovers.

The following day, over turkey, potatoes, stuffing, and everything except possibly dressing and garnish, Chuck and Brian talked for hours. Over the course of the conversation, it became increasingly clear that they were attracted to each other. Finally, one of them admitted it. Though the feeling was mutual, Chuck wasn't looking for a relationship, having been widowed a few years earlier. Brian had sympathy and respect for Chuck's situation, but he was overcome with affection, and wound up staying the night. Both of them were happy with the decision, though Chuck joked that it was presumptuous of Brian to bring a toothbrush (which he'd brought simply in preparation for a long drive).

Brian's commute became a regular occurrence, and their relationship flourished. It wasn't long before he had a toothbrush at Chuck's. The two decided to attend the annual

IAGSDC (International Association of Gay Square Dance Clubs) Convention in Portland together, and on the drive from San Francisco to Oregon, they discovered they traveled together as well as they danced. They had a blast in Portland—dancing all weekend and making new friends.

Inspired by friends' encouragement, Chuck decided, for the first time, to enter the convention's annual midnight Honky Tonk Queen contest—as he describes it, "a tongue in cheek, gender-bending 'beauty' contest with square dance elements."

Brian was already in bed, having danced nonstop the entire day, when Chuck came into their hotel room and presented him with a ripped T-Shirt, boxer shorts and a jar of soap bubbles, transforming him into an escort for Chuck's newly invented drag persona, Pasty Sue Veneer. "We went onstage in front of a thousand people and proceeded to dance," said Brian. "One drag queen had a full-blown Christmas Tree on her head." "It was my first attempt to do drag, in a ratty wig, a half-slip and makeup applied by the light of fireworks," Chuck added. They had fun, and the contest went well; it was not the last time Chuck and Brian would take the stage together to perform their John Waters– and truck stop–inspired drag act.

In 2000, Brian was awarded his PhD in English from Stanford, and Chuck was laid off, raising questions for both about the course their lives would take. Brian was offered a position as professor of English at the University of Washington, and Chuck found a new job managing corporate events in California. Faced with the prospect of living in different states, the two discussed the situation at length. Chuck stayed in California but frequently traveled for work. Brian stayed with him in California when classes weren't in session, and Chuck was sometimes able to fly to Seattle for a weekend with Brian.

After making this arrangement work for an impressive five years, Chuck and Brian were tired of missing each other so frequently. They wanted to share a home, the quiet times after work, and the minutia of daily life. They resolved to find a way to live together. Chuck sold his house, put all but the necessities in storage, and moved into Brian's apartment (the dimensions of which Chuck described by pantomiming an area the size of a walnut). With luck and some searching, they found a house in Seattle the perfect size for themselves and their cat, Sam; their first home together.

Fortuitously, after the move, Washington State redefined its domestic partnership, granting partnered residents nearly all of the legal rights of married ones. Without question, Brian and Chuck knew they loved each other, and decided it was time to take a huge step and register for a domestic partnership. "We were thrilled that we now had legal protections of medical decisions, rights of inheritance, and health insurance," said Chuck.

When DOMA was overturned, Chuck was finally legally able to make one of the most profound gestures of love—he asked Brian to spend his life with him. Chuck's marriage proposal, appropriately, was made over leftovers.

Rather than quietly letting their domestic partnership transfer into a marriage license, the two decided to have a big party with friends and family.

Chuck's family, who had always been supportive of his relationship with Brian, was elated to hear they were getting married. Chuck discussed the details of the event with his mother, who helped generate ideas.

Brian and Chuck took a road trip to visit Brian's parents in Illinois, so he could talk to them about the upcoming wedding and make sure they would be part of the celebration. Happy for their son and his soon-to-be husband, they agreed to come to Seattle for what they called Brian and Chuck's "Special Day."

Chuck's background in event planning could not have been more useful in preparation for the "Special Day." He had planned many weddings, and combined the best parts of all of them to create the best celebration he could imagine. The process involved collaboration with other professional planners, who pressured Chuck and Brian to model their wedding exactly after a certain kind of traditional straight wedding. But Chuck and Brian were adamant that the celebration involve only personally significant elements. Chuck wanted their sexual identities be honored and celebrated by their wedding, rather than downplayed.

For example, rather than the flower arrangements the planners suggested, they designed decorations they felt representative of their masculinity. They gathered gourds, miniature pumpkins, and brightly colored autumn maple leaves, which Chuck's best man and his partner made into centerpieces.

Chuck and Brian chose the University of Washington Faculty Club as a venue for its lovely views and excellent food, and to show their support of the university—which was, after all, the reason for their move to Seattle.

They opted for a custom playlist rather than the traditional hired DJ. The list, compiled by Chuck, included jazz and other cocktail-party appropriate genres to set the mood for a dinner party. "We wanted people to be able to mingle without being pulled to the dance floor for the hokeypokey when they were in the midst of a great conversation," he said. In addition to DJs and flower arrangements, the two excluded the traditional bouquet and garter throwing, which they feel is sexist.

Guests were offered a variety of drinks upon their arrival, to help them get comfortable and offset the gravity of the occasion, which can border on somberness at some weddings. The playlist during this time included some tongue in cheek classics such as Grace Jones's "I Need a Man," the Weather Girls's "It's Raining Men," and Lyle Lovett's version of "Stand By Your Man," which contributed to a party atmosphere.

To commence the ceremony, Chuck and Brian made their entrance to Judy Garland's rendition of "Somewhere over the Rainbow," hand in hand, wearing matching tuxedos and purple bow ties, with tears of joy in their eyes. There were soon tears in the eyes of the guests, as well.

A mutual friend Arnie (an Internet-ordained minister) and the best men, Steve and Chris, met the couple at the front of the room, where Chuck and Brian exchanged rings. As at Chuck's traditional Thanksgiving dinners, Brian and Chuck were in the company of all the people they choose to be with, and they shared the vows they had written for each other and signed their marriage license in the presence of this beloved audience. During the ceremony, Chuck and Brian surprised the guests by producing cameras from their pockets and turning around to photograph the assembly, which reacted with laughter.

Later, Brian and Chuck were pleased to discover the caper had yielded some pretty good pictures. "Everything doesn't have to serious," said Chuck. "Weddings are a celebration; they should be fun."

The newlyweds joined their parents for an old-fashioned receiving line and welcomed everyone to the dining room to enjoy the celebratory Thanksgiving feast. They describe the rest of the day as a blur of really good memories.

Chuck and Brian had worked with the faculty club's chef to design a Thanksgiving dinner of turkey, brussels sprouts, potatoes, and pumpkin pie: an homage to their first autumn together and the shared values symbolized by the holiday. The dinner was a hit; the turkey even seduced one vegetarian.

At dinner, toasts from the best men (each a friend of Chuck and Brian since childhood) concluded with an invitation to the guests to move to another table and meet new people, in the style of academic dinners at Oxford, where Brian was a Rhodes Scholar.

In addition to pie, dessert, of course, included wedding cake. Chuck and Brian's cake was from Morfey's Cake, a long-standing Seattle favorite. The three-tiered cake was decorated with circles, dots, and a lavender ribbon, and contained a layer of peanut butter, Chuck and Brian's favorite flavor. The cake topper: a silhouette of two men holding a tiny heart.

# BOOZE

## Paul & Philip

IN HIS LATE TEENS, PHILIP MOVED to Spokane, Washington to attend Whitworth College on a music scholarship. Paul was working as a barista at Starbucks, while attending community college with plans to pursue a degree in business. Philip had noticed Paul around town on several occasions before he worked up the courage to approach him. "I had seen him at Starbucks," said Philip. "I didn't go talk to him because it was conservative Spokane, and I was afraid I'd get killed." Philip may have also been nervous because of his strict Evangelical Christian upbringing in Canada. When he first spoke to Paul, he was still an actual choirboy. Once, having coffee with a friend while Paul was working, Philip joked that he was in love with Paul and was going to marry him.

Then, while at an after-hours shopping night at Nordstrom (the most entertaining place in quiet Spokane, Paul and Philip agree), Philip saw a server drop a tray of champagne on the stairs. Philip was about to help her clean it up when he turned around and bumped into Paul. It turned

out the friends the two were there with knew each other. Outside, they exchanged numbers. "We met outside the store. We both had the same cheap phone that looked like a peanut. The first you get when you're nineteen and it's 2003," Philip recalled.

Philip went on tour with his choir for the next week, but when he returned, it only took him and Paul a couple of weeks to realize there was something significant between them. "It was a fateful start," said Paul. "There were all these weird things that happened," Philip added. "We still have the clipping of Paul's horoscope that said he was going to meet the love of his life."

When Philip went to his parents' in Bellingham for the holidays, he told them about Paul. The reaction was nasty— they said if he continued to date a man, his stuff would be out on the lawn when he next came to visit. When Paul heard how things were going, he was in Bellingham within a few hours. "I drove a used 1981 Honda Civic," Paul said. "The entire front end was smashed. I feared for my life." He picked Philip up and drove him to his own parents' house in Graham, Washington, where they had a lovely holiday in each other's company. They realized how much they meant to each other—Philip was brave enough to tell his Evangelical Christian parents he loved Paul, and Paul dropped everything to help and comfort Philip when he had to deal with the repercussions.

Though Philip and Paul were immediately drawn to each other, and—as they put it—they're great for each other on paper, it took years for them to just enjoy hanging out together like friends—talking, doing laundry, sharing boring everyday life. "Paul was like hearts, stars, and rainbows [when we met], and I was doom and gloom," said Philip. "It's like a yin and yang sort of thing. We balance each other out. We both love art and beautiful things," Paul added.

By their early twenties, they were living in a slick loft in Seattle's Pioneer Square neighborhood. They loved to entertain, both being the sort of hosts who wouldn't hesitate to buy themed flatware for a dinner party. They had many cocktail parties, usually using what they term the "Build-a-Bear" method of drink service: they provided a bar with a wide variety of garnishes, liquors, and mixers that go well together and let guests make whatever suited their fancy. They had a "Boozy Brunch Bar" and a "Champagne Tea Party" with crumpets, tea sandwiches, and teacups of champagne. They even hosted a "Tour de Franzia" party, where guests watched the bike race while drinking every variety of Franzia boxed wine. Paul and Philip were fortunate enough to become acquainted with Rachel Marshall, creator of Rachel's Ginger Beer and co-owner of the popular Seattle bar Montana, while she was still making ginger beer in her own kitchen, so several of their parties featured her mixers.

Paul and Philip were also both the sort of people who wanted to be thirteen at seven and thirty at twenty. After six years, they shared a home and a car, and felt that it was time to get married. They were very traditional in their approach to planning. They started by informing their families, which wasn't easy, though conditions had certainly improved. "My family thought about it," said Philip. "They realized the bottom line was they really liked Paul."

To their surprise, Paul and Philip became increasingly uneasy as the wedding-planning process progressed. All of the details of the celebration were falling into place, yet they both knew something was wrong. Through a series of difficult conversations, they finally came to the conclusion that the problem was that in a way, they didn't know why they were getting married. Of course, they couldn't be together once they realized this. They had sent out all the save-the-dates and invites (of which there were nearly two hundred) when they broke up.

Philip had recently landed his first well-paying job, while Paul was still working at Starbucks. Paul felt he needed to think about what he really wanted to do. They had worked hard for everything in the life they shared, yet things normally considered milestones felt empty. They had met when they were so young that neither of them really knew who he was without the other.

The traditional trajectory of a relationship—buying a house, then a car, and then getting married—had been like checking boxes for Paul and Philip. The process of planning a wedding brought up many emotions regarding family and their future. They realized that on some level they had been going through the motions rather than having genuine experiences. They felt they had become codependent to an extent that threatened their identity as individuals. They broke up in an effort to reconnect with their individual passions, inspirations, desires, values, and feelings.

"We both worked very hard with journaling, meditating, therapy, reflecting, making art, and having meaningful conversations with friends and family, which ultimately brought us back together. Which is a common theme in our relationship," said Philip. "When we feel distant, we often realize we are on the same page or that we both want the ultimate goal but go about it in different ways. We knew why we were getting married; they just weren't the right reasons and it didn't feel authentic."

The following time apart, though lonely and scary, turned out to be a healthy decision. Philip and Paul agree therapy—and the resulting view of self-improvement as an ongoing process—has been helpful to them throughout their relationship. "We were apart three and a half months," said Philip. "We got back together because we had taken some time for ourselves and realized our codependent relationship had been version 1.0. We decided we could do it again—make it better, different, and stay better connected to ourselves." When Paul and Philip got back together, they had a much clearer understanding of why they loved each other, having experienced each other's absence.

One of the first things Paul decided was that he no longer wanted to work at Starbucks. He landed a job at the Giddens School in Seattle, where he taught a blended class of kindergarteners and first graders. Philip worked at Nordstrom for several years (which they got a kick out of, since they met there) before moving to a boutique on Capitol Hill called Totokaelo, which specializes in clothing and luxury designer products.

Paul and Philip were in the process of planning a tenth-anniversary party when, after some conversation, they realized they did actually want to exchange vows. Having made a conscious effort during the four years following their first attempt at marriage to figure out who they were and what made them happy, they planned the event much differently. Rather than simply planning as tradition dictated, they decided to incorporate only elements that were meaningful to them. "The second time we told everyone to go fuck themselves, basically," said Philip. "We didn't want some church-basement wedding," said Paul.

The pared down their guest list, inviting only people they really felt had been committed to them over the past ten years, which took the list down to eighty-five from the previous two hundred. The invitations were elegant and somewhat cryptic. They chose a venue in Leavenworth, Washington, whose citizens voted to remodel the entire town as a Bavarian village in the early 1960s—even the fast-food places resemble the lids of ornate beer steins. Philip and Paul wanted black glassware, dark linens, and flowers in shades of red and burgundy. In the past they had worried a black-tie wedding would be an inconvenience to guests, but having bought enough jet-black glassware for eighty-five people and arranged for its delivery to Leavenworth, requesting that guests rent suits seemed reasonable. Telling people to go fuck themselves, in this context, meant that Paul and Philip were going to have exactly the wedding they wanted, but what they wanted was largely the ultimate hosting gig. They wanted to show everyone they cared about a wonderful time, based on what they had learned from years of hosting parties together. "For us, having loads of booze and beautiful food was about giving back to all the people who supported us in our journey," said Philip.

Because of the wedding's faux-Bavarian setting, Paul and Philip started the evening with a pretzel bar, a sort of Teutonic carbohydrate version of the garnish and mixer buffets at their house parties, held in a gallery of artifacts and photos from Paul and Philip's ten years together. Pretzels were served with mustard made by a nearby bratwurst stand

and Kölsch from a local brewery, Icicle. Paul and Philip appeared wearing lederhosen, which cracked up the guests after the insistence on tuxes.

While the two changed into their own tuxes, dinner began, starting with Montana Mules (whiskey and ginger beer) and Mad Vatters (vodka, cranberry juice, and mandarin-orange ginger beer), mixed by Rachel, of course. Rather than a traditional wedding procession, Paul and Philip simply took their seats in the dining area. They made their entrance to a Lana Del Rey song, and then a soprano at the table ushered in every course of the wedding meal with a Schumann piece.

"The entire procession of the evening was planned so that there would never be a moment when the guests wondered what would happen next," said Philip. In the tradition of the couple's dinners and cocktail parties, every element of the wedding was designed to surprise and delight. This array of amusements included cigarettes, mints, antacids, body spray, personalized matches, and Instagram photos displayed in the bathroom. Paul even carefully constructed a wall of pretzels.

Friends read an excerpt from David Sedaris's *When You Are Engulfed in Flames*, a Clementine von Radics poem called "Mouthful of Forevers," and an excerpt about marriage from Khalil Gibran's *The Prophet*, which Philip and Paul chose partly because it's free of pronouns. As they read their vows, they were struck by how safe and loved they felt in the company they had chosen.

After toasts came the traditional dance with moms and a party during which karaoke videos were projected on the walls, eight cases of champagne were consumed, and Paul's grandma danced to Peaches's "Fuck the Pain Away." "We ran out of champagne," said Philip. "It was that kind of night. Red wine just didn't suit." Paul and Philip had reserved cabins surrounding the wedding venue so that guests could party as hard as they wanted without an ensuing struggle to figure out how to get home. It was an appropriately wild celebration for a love that had weathered two people's passage from childhood to adulthood. Philip and Paul felt the Clementine von Radics poem read during the ceremony sums up what they are together. The final lines read:

> *whether it's the days you burn*
> *more brilliant than the sun*
> *or the nights you collapse into my lap*
> *your body broken into a thousand questions,*
> *you are the most beautiful thing I've ever seen.*
> *I will love you when you are a still day.*
> *I will love you when you're a hurricane.*

# CAKES

---

## Jem & Sterling

IN 1963, JEM HAD JUST STARTED grad school at the University of Washington, and he hated everything about it. He hated the campus, he didn't know anyone, he didn't know how to get around town. One day, hoping for a distraction, he bought a ticket to *Swan Lake*. Upon returning to his car, he saw he had gotten a parking ticket. He was cursing Seattle and everything in it when he ran into Ken, a friend from undergrad at the University of Oregon, who invited him to a party at his house that night. It was going to be sort of a *Swan Lake* after-party with homemade beer. Still feeling low when he got to the party, Jem proceeded to get completely hammered. Around one in the morning, he started talking with Sterling, who had just arrived. They were talking and drinking in the kitchen when Ken walked up, put his arms around Sterling, and said, "How's my favorite cop?" When he learned Sterling was indeed a policeman, who had just gotten off his 5:00 to 1:00 a.m. shift, Jem said, "Oh God, I just told a cop I have a parking ticket!"

They had the classic postparty meal at IHOP and then went to Sterling's apartment, where Jem promptly fell asleep on the couch. The next morning, he confessed, to Sterling's amusement, that he had no idea where he was. Sterling led him to his car, which was only three blocks away. Four hours later, Jem was back. He invited Sterling to see a movie with him that night. "He was wearing a nice little blue polo shirt embroidered with an alligator, blue jeans, and white tennis shoes," said Sterling. "I said, 'Oh shit.' I was wearing the same thing!" They laughed about this and made plans to go out that evening, on the condition that one of them change his outfit first.

The movie, they still remember, was *Kind Hearts and Coronets*. They left hand in hand, neither aware of how completely they would fall in love, and how rapidly. "You'll stumble over it," Jem told me. "Don't look for love. It just happens." Jem took a teaching job in Salem, Oregon, while Sterling continued to work as a policeman by night and attend undergrad classes at UW by day. Jem drove all the way from Oregon to visit Sterling every weekend. Soon, they began looking for an apartment. After they'd been together about a year, Sterling found a little run-down house in Seattle's Ravenna neighborhood, and they bought it together.

Jem's dad had come to Washington from Iowa in the '40s to work in the shipyards but suffered a massive heart attack that rendered him unable to work. Jem and the rest of his family, including his twin brother moved into one of the hundreds of temporary homes built by the government to support industry during the '40s. Of his twin, Jem said, "He's as straight as they come, and I'm as gay as they come. I don't know how that happens." Jem did well in high school and showed particular talent for art. He would have gone on to become a commercial sign-maker if the junior college hadn't offered him a job they designed just for him: campus sign-maker. While on a scholarship at Northwest Christian College, he began attending art classes at the University of Oregon and decided he wanted to go into art education.

Sterling grew up in Tacoma, Washington, where his mother was, as he delicately put it, "a barmaid and a comfort to all of Tacoma." One day when he was fourteen, he came home from school to find a padlock on the door of their apartment. The landlord told him that his mother, whom he hadn't seen in a few days, hadn't paid the rent in months. He later found out she had gone to California with a soldier. Sterling slept on a park bench for the next three nights. Though he was only fourteen, he managed to get a job washing dishes in a coffee dive and found himself a small apartment. He learned to ride horses, well enough that he even trained a few. He wanted to go to the University of Washington, but the job he had at Boeing at the time wasn't very lucrative. Sterling's doctor, who liked him and knew he wanted to go to college, told the Seattle city treasurer, George Culver, about his predicament. Culver was moved to find Sterling a night shift with the Seattle Police Department.

By the time Jem and Sterling finished school, they both knew they wanted to be teachers. They managed to get jobs at the same junior high school. Sterling taught English, and Jem taught art. "You couldn't mention being gay if you were a teacher then," said Jem. "It was the dark ages. They were still raiding gay bars."

Jem and Sterling didn't express affection in public and didn't go to any public gay social events. They hosted quiet parties at home but never went to gay bars or anywhere else that would attract attention to their relationship, for fear of losing their jobs.

The two were aware that the other teachers had seen them arrive together in the morning. Worried by what might happen if the faculty found out they were together, they worked as hard as they could to be indispensable. They were never late, and they took on extra duties. By the time their co-workers knew they were gay, no one cared, especially not the principal. "One time I went into his office," said Sterling. "We had a parent-teacher conference. This irate woman went out all smiles. He said, 'You know what, Mr. Smith? If I could hire sixty percent gay teachers, I would. They're just better.'" On the few occasions when other faculty members brought up their relationship in an attempt to harm them professionally, the principal was quick to defend them.

Sterling and Jem did some work on a beautiful century-old house on a few acres of land in Federal Way, Washington. "We'd done some painting [for the house's owner] because he was allergic to paint. He was allergic to everything. He was kind of a funny guy. We said, if you get tired of the place, call us," said Sterling. He did get tired of it, but he set up the paperwork in such a way that he could flee to Mexico with a chunk of Jem and Sterling's money without relinquishing ownership of the house. Ownership was dependent on a payment that he assumed was too high for the couple to pay at once. He didn't realize they had sold a large portion of the antiques they'd been collecting since they met, and the payment was already made. There was no trip to Mexico for him. It was the first time Jem and Sterling had signed the title on a house together; this was a time when the legality of accepting the signatures of two men or two women on a title was questionable.

One night Jem and Sterling were watching a news special about the AIDS epidemic. There had only been a handful of cases diagnosed in the Northwest at the time. Jem was alarmed to recognize one of the patients interviewed for the special as a good friend from the University of Oregon. He and Sterling called the TV station as well as an HIV prevention and support group in New York, trying to get the man's phone number, but no one would give them his contact information. The man eventually heard they were trying to reach him, though, and called them. His wife, from whom he was separated, called Jem and Sterling on a night they had planned to come over for dinner and told them they didn't have to, because the man had just died. Stunned by the tragedy, they offered her the first gesture of kindness they could think of—a day on the town.

"That was how [Chicken Soup Brigade] got started," said Sterling. "We called and asked if the caregivers of people with AIDS needed time off. The first two times we called four and five days before they died. Some of their ashes are sprinkled near our home." Volunteers accumulated, and today the organization, based out of Seattle's Lifelong AIDS Alliance, has an average of 150 volunteers who prepare meals, bring groceries, and collect donations for people with AIDS and other illnesses. Jem and Sterling were among the organization's first volunteers.

"We did that for twenty-six years," said Sterling. "Chicken Soup turned into a big organization. They asked us if we would come in Saturdays to train volunteers. We knew what to do, what not to do, what to say. They wanted to honor [Jem and me]. We said no, we don't need it, but if it'll be a fundraiser, we'll go. When they opened the doors at the Four Seasons hotel, there were thirty tables that sat ten people each. There was this comedian who roasted us, dressed as

a nun. Those three hundred people stood and applauded. It took in $80,000."

Considering their initial feelings about their completely deserved honorary breakfast, it's unsurprising that Jem and Sterling considered a big church wedding after fifty years together "too pushy." Also, when gay marriage became legal in Washington, they were still tired from hosting their fiftieth anniversary party, where they served five huge rainbow cakes, one for each decade they had been together. The love that Jem and Sterling had to hide for the majority of those years was celebrated by over two hundred people—enough to eat all five cakes.

Only a dozen guests were invited to Jem and Sterling's wedding in Federal Way, where they lived with their dogs, chickens, and a very old horse who enjoys classical music. Jem and Sterling added new rooms to the house after outwitting its questionable former owner in the '70s and filled them with art and antiques. Cases of Wedgwood pottery line the walls like an Egyptian tomb's treasure. They were married by a judge in front of their own fireplace. "He wrote everything for it," said Sterling. "He really did a nice job."

Afterward Jem, Sterling, and their twelve guests had dinner at Black Angus. In this small-town strip-mall steak house, Jem and Sterling had one of a growing number of experiences that reflect increasing acceptance and even appreciation of same-sex relationships. After so many years forced to keep their love as private as possible, such interactions shocked them and filled them with joy. When the waitress brought the bill, she commented on the celebratory mood of the party and asked if there was an occasion. When Sterling told her that he and Jem had just been married after fifty-one years together, her eyes filled with tears. So did theirs.

## POSTSCRIPT

When I called Jem and Sterling a month after our interview to ask for a photo of them together, Jem told me Sterling had just died. I couldn't believe it—it seemed I'd just been eating carrot cake with the charming man, who had aged in such a way his features only seemed to show lines from smiling, in his living room hours ago. Before I even felt anything, tears were running down my face. The thought of Jem alone in their house was awful to me. Jem actually apologized for upsetting me with the news, which stunned me further.

I asked to meet up with Jem for lunch. He talked about how intelligent Sterling was, how he had a particular faculty for language, how he loved flowers and knew their botanical names, and how one of the saddest things is having to look words up in the dictionary now that Sterling is no longer around to spell them for him. The collection of antiques in their home was Sterling's hobby; he filled their lives with beautiful things. When Jem landscaped their property, Sterling plotted out its design.

Jem showed me the obituary he had written for Sterling, part of which read:

> Sterling passed away Dec. 2, 2014, due to a heart condition. He leaves behind his partner of 51 years Jem, his stepmother Anne, two great dogs, and hundreds of friends. He was beloved by all who know him and will be greatly missed! He was known as an outstanding effective teacher and was highly respected by both colleagues and students. Sterling and Jem were caregivers for 37 AIDS patients over 22 years. Sterling loved teaching, reading, gardening, landscaping, cooking, music, the arts, antique buying and selling, and most of all Christmas when he could decorate and give gifts. Sterling will be fondly remembered by his many friends for his gracious hospitality, good humor, and engaging interest in others.

When I asked Jem how he was doing, he said he was having a hard time but his friends were keeping him busy, which made me happy—I hope that a person with such strength and compassion will never be lonely. I cried when I heard Sterling had died, but then I realized he was eighty-two. He had a life full of adventure, his work had saved people's lives, and he shared a beautiful house and art with a guy who loved him and was good to him for over fifty years. He won.

# MUSIC

## Doug & Randy

IN 1998, DOUG POSTED A PERSONAL ad in search of a man who shared his love of romance, adventure, and martinis. Randy, who found all of these appealing (who wouldn't, really?) quickly responded to the ad. After a long phone conversation during which they discussed the big issues, such as whether it's best to pee over the top of underwear or through the fly (a matter they wholeheartedly agree on—in Randy's words, "Who pushes their wiener through the underwear? It's weird. You have to unfold them like origami."), they went out for Thai food. As soon as Doug got in Randy's car, he had the fabled moment of immediately knowing a person is important. Doug was sick and had to fly to Europe the following morning, so Randy went to Bartell Drugs and bought him a tiny bottle of cold medicine, which he had the cashier put in an absurdly huge bag that might have been more appropriate for a small appliance. Doug laughed, and was smitten—he may have broken his rule against kissing on the first date.

Doug originally began to think about settling down at thirty (five years before he met Randy), but his hairdresser had advised him to wait until thirty-five. "So I went to Key West by myself," Doug said, "and got everything out of my system, and then some." "I have pictures!" Randy added.

The first time Randy came to Doug's, he saw a photo on the wall of a woman doing "something questionable" with a champagne bottle. "I asked, 'Who's that pretty woman?'" Randy recalled. "He said, 'Me!' I knew I was in for the ride of my life."

Doug got into the Seattle drag scene after winning the Queen of Hearts pageant in 1984. His success as a drag queen actually outed him to his family. He was in a theater company called Greek Active that put on *The Children's Hour*, a play about two lesbian school teachers. Doug's mom saw a picture of him in full drag on the cover of the paper, and soon they were having an uncomfortable phone conversation. "Her first question was 'How do you decide who's the man and who's the woman?'" Doug said. "She has come such a long way. If I had ever dreamed she would be the maid of honor at my marriage to another man, I'd have laughed."

As it turned out, Doug and Randy both love drag. They've now seen every John Waters movie, two of their favorite drag queens being Divine and Dina Martina. Doug was delighted when he found out Randy can do the Mashed Potato as well as anyone in *Hairspray*. They sometimes put on Dee Dee Sharp's "Mashed Potato Time" when friends are over so Randy can show off his skills.

Doug has had enough jobs to write a book about them, but he loves his current job at a corporate office supporting an assisted-living community. Randy, who grew up in Eureka, California, and moved to Washington to attend travel school, has been a travel agent ever since, scoring deals like seventy-five-dollar round-trip flights to Amsterdam. They've been all over the world together, and their yard is decorated with souvenirs from their travels, like the Mayan calendar on the fence and homages to it, such as a pineapple plant to remind them of Hawaii (which they admit is actually from Safeway).

Two months after their first date, they were more or less living together on Capitol Hill. They listened to a lot of Savage Garden, and "Truly Madly Deeply" became their song. Doug helped Randy move into a neighboring apartment, but the two spent so much time at Doug's that Randy's things stayed in boxes. During the moving process, Doug met Randy's friend Laurie—the woman who would one day officiate their wedding. At first, they had their differences. "I wanted to put his rosemary pot on my balcony," Doug said, "but she wanted that rosemary, and she pulled one of many *he's been my friend for longer*s." Randy was in France with Laurie when he was unexpectedly seized by the fear that Doug might go back to his ex. This was before the era of cell phones—Randy's frantic walk through the streets of Paris in search of a pay phone concluded with the discovery that he had no idea how to operate a French pay phone. When Randy finally managed to make the call, Doug told him he had no intention of being with anyone but Randy. Not long afterward, Doug told Randy he loved him, and the sentiment was returned.

Besides the resolution of rosemary-related conflicts and general integration of the groups of people the couple love, little has changed since the quest for romance, adventure, and martinis began. When I asked what they most like to do together, Doug said, "Nothing!" "We like to lounge in the pool, have friends over," said Randy. "Randy convinced me to try pot," Doug said, "and I got Randy hooked on musical theater. Though I think we've left more shows at intermission than we've sat through." "Because they sucked!" said Randy. "*Lion King* sucked!" Their favorite show by far is *Oklahoma!*. They've been to Disneyland several times, and since they always go on the "It's a Small World" ride first, the song, amusingly, has become imbued with romantic significance for them.

There seems to be little the two disagree about, besides brussels sprouts and clams, and they still attempt to appreciate these things for each other's sake. "We've never had a fight," Randy told me. "Most people think we're freaks, but no, it's because I love him. I would never think of doing any-thing mean or hurtful to him."

This attitude toward disagreement may have yielded the most lovely moment of their wedding. It was one of several grand surprises that day, the biggest being the ceremony itself. Doug wrote in his invitation to me (I was invited so that I could write about the event for Wedding Crasher), "Everyone except our mothers, and the officiant, a good friend ordained online [Laurie], and now you—thinks we got married on July 5th under the ruse that we are far too weepy to get through it in front of everyone. Which we are. We are going to surprise them all and really get married at what they think is just the reception."

Doug and Randy's domestic partnership would have transferred into a marriage license automatically when gay marriage passed in Washington, but they wanted to cele-brate what was approaching two happy decades together—as did their friends and family, who know the kind of parties the two are capable of throwing.

Preparation for the poolside wedding at their home in Shoreline, Washington, took about two months and $5,000. Doug hadn't yet begun work at the assisted-living commu-nity, so conveniently he had lots of time to plan. Several ele-ments of the wedding were inspired by the couple's annual trips to Hawaii. Doug hired Shooby Doo Catering to design a menu incorporating Spam, which Randy loves, and Doug's favorite, corn dogs. The menu was meant to be a surprise for Randy, but Doug soon told him, because he couldn't bear keeping so many secrets at once.

Appropriately for a couple whose wedding playlist ranged from Sara Bareilles to polka, the final surprise was musical. The first time Doug and Randy saw a mariachi band was at a restaurant called Pipi's in Puerto Vallarta. Doug didn't care for them ("I was like, bleh!" he said of the experience), but Randy adored them in a way that made Doug happy to witness, and that stayed in his memory. About five people knew the two would actually be exchanging vows at the reception, but only Doug and his friend Michelle knew about the musical surprise that would follow the ceremony.

When the day arrived, over forty friends and family members gathered in Doug and Randy's backyard. Only a few people the couple had hoped to see at their wedding were unable to attend. The biggest disappointment was the absence of Randy's mom, whose move to Seattle was hindered by health issues. It was a move, though, not a visit, so they would have plenty of time to celebrate with her later (which they since have). The couple ordered enough leis to fill their refrigerator, and the entire yard smelled of plumeria. The mix of songs playing was among the most delightful and eclectic collections of music I've heard. If there was a "Doug and Randy's Favorites" box set, I would buy it. It included Sara Bareilles's "I Choose You," written for queer weddings, and a song by a long-dead Hawaiian singer who could carry a note like her lungs were inflatable air mattresses. Randy mentioned they've made a game of trying to hold bong hits for the length of a note. They told me they'd spent a lot of time choosing songs that are important. It was a kind of musical mosaic of their lives together. It wasn't just a collection of songs about love—the songs were love songs in the sense that the couple had heard them at moments when they recognized their love for each other: big moments, idiosyncratic moments, quiet moments at home.

"We love Divine," said Randy. "We love yodeling. This list we played at our wedding—there's organ music and mariachi music. We appreciate weird shit. We acknowledge the fact we're weird, but you wouldn't know it if you saw us walking down the street. We went to the John Waters Christmas show." "We love Dina Martina," Doug added. "We've missed maybe one show." The two excitedly recollected a Dina Martina Christmas show finale that involved the stuffing of the drag chanteuse—dressed as a turkey—with a variety of oversized plush vegetables.

Placed conveniently next to the corn dogs, coconut shrimp, and homemade POG mimosas was a bowl of joints, each tied with a dainty green bow. Doug's mom decided to celebrate the event by partaking of this party favor for the first time in her life. "It was octogenarian peer pressure," said Randy. "Her friends were smoking it!" She appeared to be having a wonderful time. The guests reclined among conch shells, tiki torches, and multicolored beach balls that looked like the aftermath of a tropical New Year's balloon drop.

The reaction to the announcement that the couple was actually exchanging vows at the party was general delight—many of those in attendance had been disappointed when they thought they had missed the ceremony. The guests left their towels and deck chairs, as if leaning out apartment windows to watch an approaching parade. Doug and Randy requested that no one make a toast—they were afraid of becoming too emotional. "I cry at Hallmark cards," Randy admitted.

The ceremony was modeled after the one in the movie *Spaceballs*," Laurie said only "Do you?" and the grooms simply responded, "I do." The assembly applauded. The ceremony's brevity didn't prevent anybody from, as Doug put it, "getting weepy." Perhaps it was the applause that prevented anyone from noticing the sound of the mariachi band warming up in the driveway. I first mistook the sound of their approach for a passing car's stereo.

When the musicians appeared, Randy put his arm around Doug, teary eyed. It was his favorite moment of the day. "There is a photo of my jaw dropping," he said. Doug's favorite moment was his realization, after getting dressed for the wedding, that he was actually marrying the man of his dreams.

## A SAMPLE OF DOUG AND RANDY'S
## WEDDING PLAYLIST:

- "Alika" by Aunty Genoa Keawe: Keawe is a Hawaiian falsetto artist with an impressive lung capacity.

- "Mashed Potato Time" by Dee Dee Sharp: This song is a favorite because it's from John Waters's Hairspray and because of Randy's ability to do the accompanying dance.

- "I Choose You" by Sara Bareilles: Doug first heard "I Choose You," his and Randy's "new" song, on the Today show when he was at home and not working. It was written specifically for same-sex couples getting married. "The words are perfect. It still makes us all weepy when we hear it!" said Doug.

- "Oh, What a Beautiful Morning" by James Taylor: This is Doug and Randy's favorite version of a song from *Oklahoma!*. In addition to putting it on the wedding playlist, they listened to it together the morning of the wedding.

- "It's a Small World" by Kitten: Doug and Randy played a yodeled version of the song from their favorite Disneyland ride. "We chose this version to make people go WTF? Also for our friend and officiant, Laurie," Doug explained.

- "Tico Tico" by Ethel Smith: Doug and Randy's friend Lori introduced them to this weird organ solo from an Esther Williams movie. They describe it as odd, fun, and hard to explain.

- "We've Only Just Begun" by the Carpenters: "Because!" said Doug.

- "Dive in the Pool" by Barry Harris and Pepper MaShay: Doug found this one while looking for fun dance music. It's high-energy gay disco from the TV series *Queer as Folk*. Randy hated it at first, but now he loves it!

- "Get the Party Started" by P!nk. Doug and Randy often hear this song at karaoke at a dive called Uncle Tim's near their cabin in Chelan, Washington. One night the hostess, Marilyn, had clogs and kept shuffling out of them. Whenever Doug and Randy trip or lose a shoe, they call it a "Marilyn."

- "Le Freak" by Chic: This was for Doug and Randy's friend Suzanne. The song is standard on their playlists. "I remember every move of a routine she did in high school to this song," said Doug. "Unfortunately she wouldn't do it at the party!"

- "Truly Madly Deeply" by Savage Garden: Doug and Randy's song when they first met.

# TOASTS

WHILE READING LAST DAYS (David Schmader's tragic, hilarious, and morbid news column in the *Stranger*), Jake would often tell a friend at work, "He should be my boyfriend." He was walking near the *Stranger* offices with a friend of his, DJ Freddy, King of Pants, one night when they saw David across the street. "Hey, it's David Schmader," yelled Freddy. "No, you're David Schmader!" David yelled back. He invited the two up to his office, where they smoked a lot of weed. Jake was thrilled—not only was he in his local celebrity crush's office, but he had also met a man who got to smoke weed in his office. Dave offered Jake and Freddy a ride home. Jake felt prom-night faint when Dave dropped Freddy off first and they were alone in the car together. When they pulled up, Dave leaned over and kissed him. There was more kissing at Jake's, until Dave told him he liked him too much to go further until they'd had a proper date.

They had a series of excellent dates over the next month. Jake couldn't believe he was seeing the guy he'd jokingly called his perfect boyfriend, with no idea they would ever even speak to each other. Dave couldn't believe the hottest person he had ever dated was also the funniest. Then, something awful happened.

Dave had had a few adventures since his last relationship ended (notably one that involved blasting the *Sound of Music* soundtrack from a car at an infamous cruising spot), but he'd always been safe. He had safe sex, got tested regularly, and really didn't do anything reckless. His HIV diagnosis came as a complete shock. Friends gathered at Dave's apartment, knowing sometimes the best that can be done for someone in these situations is to offer company. Someone brought him a cake with the words "Oh fuck" written on it in frosting.

The preceding month had been one of the happiest of Dave's life, and he was convinced that happiness would end when he told Jake. He was terrified. The illness seemed like too much for such a new relationship to withstand. When he told Jake his diagnosis, he made it clear he would completely understand if Jake wanted to leave him. Jake felt deflated—he was frightened for Dave and for himself. But he was crazy about Dave. The conversation ended with his assurance "I'm not going to run away just because you have slut cancer."

That expression of sincerest commitment through darkest humor embodies Dave and Jake's bond on many levels. "We bullshit about what's most important," said Dave. "For secular people, our defense mechanisms are the closest thing we have to religion, so when you meet someone with the same defense mechanisms, it's like meeting someone from the same religion."

Jake grew up Mormon in Alaska. There just wasn't any place for homosexuality in the culture that surrounded him—the only sexual desire between people of the same gender he heard about manifested itself in ways that were violent and ugly. At thirteen, he was caught attempting suicide and sent to a "reparative" therapy facility. "They drugged the shit out of me," he recalls. Of course the drugs did nothing. Jake wasn't depressed; he was just gay. When he returned from the facility, he saw the first signs of his family's acceptance of his sexuality—they no longer insisted he go to church. Over the years, they have grown to accept him. In fact, most of them have since left the Mormon church.

Dave describes his experience of growing up in Texas as an "old-timey gay childhood," meaning that one waited until college to even consider coming out and felt fortunate not to be dragged behind a truck. "It was the Morrissey generation," he said. "Gay pride was like, I'm made of poison, but I'm fabulous." He knew he was gay from a very young age and easily picked up on cultural attitudes toward homosexuality at the time. "This was the 1980s, when even 'progressive' books like *Everything You Always Wanted to Know about Sex* considered homosexuals disordered freaks. So I figured my future held nothing but alcoholism, truck-stop restrooms, and overdressed poodles." Suspecting that Dave was gay or at least bisexual, his mom offered support, but as he had seen no evidence that his life could be happy and fulfilling, he suffered from a persistent sense of hopelessness.

When Dave asked Jake what he'd like to do on their second date, Jake suggested an interstate killing spree. Dave was instantly seduced. Like many incredibly funny people, Dave and Jake had been through some rough times. Humor and irony can create the emotional distance necessary to get through real hardship. The two could sense the emotional subtexts of each other's jokes and recognize another intelligent, sensitive person as tough as a brick shithouse.

In 2008, Jake and Dave went to California to see a stage production of Dolly Parton's *9 to 5*. They happened to be there during a brief window of time when gay marriage was legal in the state. When Jake learned of this, he asked Dave, via text, if he wanted to get married. Dave said yes immediately. They'd been together seven years, and there was no one else either of them would rather be with, but the lack of hesitation was partly because they had both come to regard events in a certain emotional register as grand jokes. They made plans to get their marriage license from the courthouse where O. J. Simpson was acquitted for murder, then called their families to tell them the news.

When their parents heard, they flew across the country. Suddenly, the marriage was real to Dave and Jake. It wasn't that the couple had previously doubted their love for each other, but growing up, they had both trained themselves not to expect the kind of relationship they had. They certainly never expected to marry anyone.

Jake's dad was ordained by the Universal Life Church, which he saw an ad for in the back of *Rolling Stone*, so that he could be their officiant. "In Mormonism, you're not even supposed to acknowledge other religions exist," said Dave, "so that's like, punk." They planned to have dinner with their parents at an Italian restaurant in Beverly Hills. Upon their arrival, they found that Dave's brother, who couldn't be there that night, had ordered them a bottle of champagne. Jake's dad wrote a communal, spiritual accompaniment to the legal part of Dave and Jake's ceremony. He read the lyrics of Ella Fitzgerald's "My Romance" and cried. So did everyone else. "My dad is German," said Dave, "so he doesn't show emotion unless he's drunk or there's a war." The great importance of the evening for Dave's and Jake's families made the couple realize how important it was to the two of them, as well as how important they actually were to each other. Before signing their marriage contract, they had a bachelor party at Jumbo's Clown Room, a Beverly Hills strip club originally owned by a Barnum & Bailey clown, where Courtney Love used to strip.

Jake and Dave's friends were as excited as their parents when they heard the news that they were married, and it became clear that a reception party in Seattle was in order.

In April, Dave and Jake decided the Valley School in Seattle's Madison Valley would be host to the party. The Valley School had a big courtyard for their friends' many kids to run around in and several comfortable old farmhouses where the party could migrate if it rained. The night before the reception, they had a wildly successful second bachelor party (*Showgirls* themed—Dave is famous for his live commentary on the film) at which Jake's Mormon grandma got drunk for the first time in her life.

Happily, the reception fell on the first really warm day of spring, and Jake bought enough tulips to fill a car. Friends and family cooked all the food and helped the newlyweds arrange their homemade decorations. Upon noticing the kids playing in the courtyard, neighbors led in a horse, a goat, and several chickens, delighting and confusing the already delighted and somewhat confused guests (some drinking had been going on). Dave's and Jake's families began a round of toasts, inspiring tears and applause. Once family had given their congratulations and raised their glasses, Dave and Jake's friend Barry made a toast. There was something familiar about Barry's choice of words—Dave and Jake soon recognized it as (hilariously) a recitation of Whitney Houston's "I Will Always Love You." No sooner had they realized this than another friend interrupted Barry with a song. One after another, Dave and Jake's friends serenaded them with pop love songs, including *The Love Boat* theme,

Paul McCartney's "Silly Love Songs," the Magnetic Fields' "When My Boy Walks Down the Street," Elvis's "I Can't Help Falling in Love with You," and "Hopelessly Devoted to You" from *Grease*. The medley culminated with a group number that had been rehearsed by half of those in attendance. If, on the 1–10 scale of excitement about weddings, sending the marrying couple a toaster is a 4, their friends' medley of pop songs (which include kazoo instrumental breaks) was at least an 11. The volley of toasts was essentially Dave and Jake's ceremony. "There are few things I love like normal people singing," said Dave. "Non-singers busting out in song is a fast track to my emotions. Second, people are fucking busy all the time, and that such a good number of friends met twice for pre-wedding rehearsals makes me want to cry." Which he did, as did Jake, and everyone else at the wedding.

Jake and Dave realized they were expected to say something. Perhaps awed that they were in a happy relationship and that they had actually had a wedding—one that didn't even involve truck-stop bathrooms or overdressed poodles— the two hadn't prepared anything to say to each other at the reception. They were surprised and touched by how much everyone wanted to hear some words about their relationship, to hear how they loved each other. So they said just what they felt. There was applause, and they saw their happiness reflected back and multiplied by a room full of people who had always wanted that for them.

# DANCING

## Tom & Garth

PERUSING DATING SITES ONE DAY, TOM found Garth—handsome, promisingly articulate, and—he quickly discovered—a music nerd like himself. Tom was eighteen and had just moved to Seattle. They made plans to see Imperial Teen and Cibo Matto play at an all-ages club called RKCNDY. Garth, in his thirties at the time, was friends with members of Imperial Teen and decided to go to their twenty-one-and-over show the night after instead of the all-ages show, so the date fell through. Tom was disappointed but didn't think much about it. He met another guy, with whom he soon moved to Europe to escape the Bush administration. This turned out not to be the romantic adventure Tom had hoped for, and after three years, when their relationship was falling apart, they returned to Seattle.

Tom hadn't been back in town long when he was out at the Cuff one night and saw a cute guy looking at him. Garth's endearingly similar account was "I rarely went out and saw this cute boy looking at me." They started talking, and Tom recognized Garth. The two look a bit similar, stocky guys with thick red beards and glasses. They're often asked if they're brothers, and Garth is tempted to say that they're not, though they have shared DNA.

They were delighted they'd run into each other. Conversation turned into making out, and they alternated between these for the rest of the night. When Tom left Garth's apartment, Garth gave him his number on a *Buffy the Vampire Slayer* temporary tattoo. Tom was amused and charmed. He was still living with his ex, who wanted to work things out, but he couldn't stop thinking about Garth. "I liked him so much, I did everything I could to get my ex out of my place," said Tom. Garth, who had just been dumped rather harshly, had a wild weekend in Portland to put the breakup out of his mind and then went on another date with Tom. They went to a queer night that musician Bob Mould (of Hüsker Dü and Sugar) put together at a club called the Crocodile, where they finally did get to see Imperial Teen together. They danced and drank and had a blast; the date entirely made up for the one they had missed three years before. They started going to shows together nearly every week. It's impossible to tell sometimes whether coincidences make things seem meant to happen, or if they're actually so meant to happen, it seems like coincidence, but neither of them could believe they'd run into each other again.

At the time, Garth was working at a law firm. He grew up in Michigan, just outside Detroit. He went to the University of Michigan for comparative literature and has mainly worked in law since then. He is now a paralegal at Amazon.

Tom was born in Washington, DC, but raised in Alaska, where his parents made a comfortable living as government employees. "It was easy," he said, "very middle class." He was out in high school and had a long-distance boyfriend he'd met over the Internet. As a teenager he was allowed to visit the boy in Missouri whenever finances permitted. He moved to Seattle when he found a job at a call center and now manages drug studies.

When Tom and Garth met—some would count it as the second time they met—Garth was in the process of buying a house. He and Tom had been seeing each other for only a month when Garth learned his dad's health was deteriorating. He rushed to Michigan, and Tom stayed alone in Garth's new house. At night in the house with only two cats for company, he thought about his life and what had brought him there, and realized how much he cared about Garth. Tragically, Garth's dad passed away soon after Garth arrived in Michigan. Tom offered the best anyone can give at these times, his love and company.

They went to the funeral in Michigan together. Garth's family was aware that he liked men, but Tom was the first boyfriend they'd met. Though this was awkward for them, and the circumstances were far from ideal, they recognized that he was a comfort to Garth. "At the funeral several folks from the community asked if we were business partners," Tom recalled. "After that, I was part of the family." The way things transpired after Garth lost his father proved that they could rely on each other. Upon their return to Seattle, Tom moved in with Garth.

That year, following the stress of buying a house and the death of his father, Garth lost his job. Then Tom lost his job. "I think that the way we learned to work with each other and keep each other afloat when times were bad made the rest of the times easier," said Garth. They went to rock shows and bought records even when they were broke, and they found that crises were easier in each other's company, fun things were more fun, and life was just better. It is said that the right relationships, the lasting ones, make life easier. Perhaps the romance of lovely and eerie coincidence, whether it was fate or probability, as well as this kind of ease, are both hallmarks of true love.

"We don't have any big disagreements," said Garth, "but usually they happen when we're hungry." When they were having trouble communicating, they went to a relationship counselor trained by psychologist John Gottman. They highly recommend Gottman's book *The Seven Principles for Making Marriage Work*. They are not the only one of the many couples I talked to who urge anyone in a relationship to get over couples counseling's dorky stigma and try it, at least once.

Tom and Garth decided to employ their impressive record collections and encyclopedic knowledge of music as DJs. Tom played at a bar called the Bus Stop on Sundays as DJ Hit and Run. He and Garth started a dance night, Double Dip, at a club called Re-bar. They deejayed together, billing themselves as Gin and Tonic. Bands played at Double Dip, with Gin and Tonic deejaying between sets and closing out the evening. The monthly dance night kicked off with a Bastille Day party. "No one else had a French-themed party!" said Tom.

Tom and Garth had been together ten years when gay marriage became legal in Washington. As soon as they found out the laws were changing, they decided to get married. "I remember the day DOMA fell, the added gravitas. There's not an excuse anymore; I now have the rights and responsibilities of a married American citizen," said Tom.

Garth got a terrible flu the day before the Seattle courthouse opened its doors for same sex weddings. Couples lined up to get married at midnight, but Garth was so sick he and Tom decided it would be best for him to sleep a few hours before they made their trek to the judge. Tom woke him up at four in the morning, and they drove downtown together, through quiet predawn streets. Despite Garth's illness, they felt something like the excitement on late-night car rides to the airport for long-awaited vacations. They walked through the building's halls, empty except for drifts of confetti, rice, and flower petals from the day's celebrations. "The courthouse employees had been up all night," said Tom. "They were all so tired, but so happy."

Tired and happy themselves, Tom and Garth went to an all-night diner for breakfast before work. They exchanged Ring Pops as engagement rings and still keep them in their freezer like a good-luck slice of wedding cake. Soon afterward, Garth bought Tom the wedding rings he had always wanted—from Tiffany. They got matching skull tattoos from one of their favorite artists, Lisa Orth.

After Tom and Garth were legally married, they wanted a big party, and as they had regular deejaying gigs at a legendary gay bar, Pony, they decided that would be the perfect venue. The owner, Marcus, a friend of theirs, welcomed the idea of hosting their reception. They knew that at Pony's weekly Sunday dance party, World's Tiniest Tea Dance, their favorite photographer in town, Kelly O, would be out with her camera and their favorite DJ, El Toro and Freddy, King of Pants, would be playing. "Our biggest expense was pizza and cupcakes," said Tom. They chose their friend Victoria, who was already ordained, as an officiant and their friends John and Stephanie as witnesses. They announced the wedding and invited all of their loved ones, but on such short notice, their out-of-state family members couldn't make it. Nonetheless, they were delighted and sent their congratulations.

The Tea Dance began in the early afternoon, but Tom and Garth waited until around six o'clock, when a crowd had gathered, for their ceremony. The entire Capitol Hill neighborhood had a holiday atmosphere. Tom and Garth knew of two other couples marrying in their favorite bars that night. As if gay marriage wasn't enough, marijuana had been legalized in the same election. Tom and Garth arrived to find the guys at Pony had decorated the bar for their wedding, the first ever held there. Tom is a member of a Seattle Sounders fan club called Gorilla FC, and one of his friends showed up in the club's trademark gorilla suit.

Tom and Garth ascended to Pony's kitchen table–sized stage, and Victoria made a brief, touching speech and pronounced them married. The packed bar went wild. The DJ put on an Imperial Teen song, and everyone danced. "From there, it was a blur of champagne and photo-booth photos," said Tom. The party was as much fun as any they'd danced at or deejayed in their decade together. Go-go boys danced on the bar, and Tom and Garth danced with each other, their friends, and a gorilla until the owner turned the lights up at last call.

# WEDDING GIFTS

## Jenna & Amanda

IN THE FEW HOURS AMANDA MANAGED to squeeze into her life for fun while studying art history at Macalester College in Saint Paul, Minnesota, she liked to play Dungeons & Dragons and other tabletop role-playing games. The year 2001 was a time of unprecedented busyness for her, a full-time student working up to thirty hours a week. She was dating her high school sweetheart—a solid long-standing relationship that everyone who knew Amanda expected would end in marriage. One night her roommate told her she should meet her awesome friend Jenna from high school. She too found Jenna to be awesome—after their first game of D&D, the two quickly became close friends.

They played tabletop games, got tattoos and piercings together, and confided in each other about everything. They discovered they had a variety of unlikely things in common—for instance, they'd obsessed over the same series of fantasy books, Susan Cooper's The Dark Is Rising. They both loved anime. Both continued to enjoy Dungeons & Dragons into adulthood, a fact that they often joked about.

After graduation, Amanda began a tour of jobs in Minnesota related to her degree. She worked for an art consultant and several sculptors, and began writing art criticism. "I got involved in the art-critic circle in the Twin Cities," she said. "It was a lot of fun." During this time, she and Jenna became roommates.

Jenna didn't really know what she was doing yet. She'd had a bad time in college, with the exception of a surreal year studying art in Japan. The general lousiness was exacerbated by a chronic illness that made everything tiring and difficult, and at one point necessitated a long stay in her parents' basement.

For years Amanda and her boyfriend's eventual marriage had been a given. When he actually proposed in 2006, she had to reexamine their relationship and how she felt about the prospect of a life with him. They had both changed since high school, and when Amanda thought of marrying him, she had a sinking feeling that she couldn't place. "I got a message saying, 'I want to talk to you,'" Jenna recalled. "We were in the middle of getting wrist tattoos, and she said, 'Maybe I can just divorce him later!'" Jenna gently suggested that if Amanda was having that thought, she probably shouldn't agree to marriage. Soon afterward, Amanda ended the first major relationship of her life.

Amanda and Jenna began spending a lot of time together after the breakup. They went for a walk late one night. It was snowing. When they described that walk, neither of them could recall exactly what was said, but they remembered an intense feeling that something between them had changed. "It was some kind of zeitgeist," said Amanda, "when we were out walking and came back. It all happened at once. We have since talked about moments in our friendship when we knew there was something more there, which wasn't examined at the time." "It was one of those things that creep in," Jenna added. "Each of those awkward hand-holding moments . . . I wasn't just seeking comfort; I had feelings for her."

At moments when they thought of each other as more than friends, what scared them was the possibility of unwanted advances ruining their friendship. Essentially, they both feared losing each other more than anything. They found themselves making an unusual transition straight from friendship to a committed relationship. Amanda and Jenna knew it was absolutely the right choice—the awkwardness of doing things couples do for the first time was more amusing than anything else. "I remember the first time I clumsily asked, 'Do you want to really go *out*?'" said Jenna.

That winter Jenna did lights and sound for a play at a community theater. Amanda still remembers how frightening and wonderful it was to bring her roses on opening night—the first flowers she ever gave Jenna. "I figured everyone there would know they were the first by my incredible blush," said Amanda.

They waited a little while before telling anyone besides a few close friends. Jenna wasn't too worried about her parents' reaction—Jenna's only concern was that her parents would be ostracized in conservative Rochester, Minnesota. "I call it Crotchfester for a reason," said Jenna. "My parents did lose a few friends because they were accepting of our relationship."

Amanda's parents had really liked her high school sweetheart, and they were disappointed that she wasn't marrying him. Amanda had always known she was attracted to both men and women, but she had never been in a relationship with a woman before Jenna. Her parents had trouble grasping the idea that people don't have to be exclusively straight or gay. They liked Jenna, though, and could see that she and Amanda were happy together. Ultimately, only a few Evangelical Christian members of Amanda's extended family were against her relationship with Jenna.

In the summer of 2007, Jenna and Amanda went to Appleton, Wisconsin, for a short getaway. They took a walk together one night and sat by Lake Superior. They saw a hummingbird moth like a living parasol, so big and delicate they could hardly believe it was real. It was there that Amanda gave Jenna a ring she had bought in Montreal, a symbol of their long-standing wish to always be in each other's lives.

When Amanda broke up with her fiancé, Jenna's mom offered Amanda a place to live. A few month later, Amanda and Jenna moved to Seattle together. They found a job managing a low-income apartment building for artists, and Jenna went back to school for design at Seattle Central Community College. In 2008, they got a Washington domestic partnership. "We became card-carrying lesbians by getting our domestic partnership cards," said Jenna. They both laughed.

They knew they wanted a commitment ceremony; the decision to call it that was conscious, since at the time they couldn't legally marry. Their initial intention was for it to be "small and not a big deal," on a friend's land in Payson, Illinois. Their mothers were all for the location but not so much for the small and not a big deal part. "My mom balked at the lack of dress code," said Jenna. "She said, 'What if people want to wear heels?' I said, "People will be stepping over cow pies!'" They ended up being grateful for planning help from their excited moms, who thought of details like the necessity for bathrooms.

Amanda and Jenna were not surprised by the generosity of their friends and family, but they were still overwhelmed. The manager of a tapas restaurant where they'd had one of their first dates donated all the wine for the celebration, and friends who couldn't be there made an elaborate and beautiful cake. The wedding was a potluck, but a friend volunteered to cook a main course on the spot. Jenna's aunt Connie paid for part of the cost of hiring a photographer.

Connie is a weaving reenactor—essentially a weaving historian. For the wedding, she researched handfasting, a ceremony requiring two bands, which she wove in an ancient Celtic style incorporating a sacred design called a God's eye.

In a field at the center of the property, encircled by woods, bagpipes played as Jenna and Amanda and their friends and family gathered for the ceremony. A close family friend who had known Jenna since she was a child had traveled there to speak. Jenna and Amanda's hands were wrapped in Connie's woven bands (which now hang on the wall in their home), and then they exchanged the wooden rings they had commissioned especially for the occasion.

Amanda was surprised and touched to see members of the conservative Evangelical Christian branch of her family at the wedding, given how some of them had reacted when they discovered she was with Jenna. They had even brought their kids. Overall, Jenna and Amanda couldn't believe how many people were there. "It was great to look around and see we really have a community," said Jenna.

As the sun went down, a reception-party bonfire was lit in the field, and guests drank and talked late into the night. The owner of the land had a collection of Amish buggies, and his wedding surprise was to deliver Amanda and Jenna to their VW bus honeymoon suite by horse and carriage. As the party retired, rain fell, which is considered good luck the evening of a wedding.

The following morning, Amanda and Jenna stoked the smoldering remains of the fire to make campfire coffee. A cousin of Amanda's, among the unlikelier guests, presented her and Jenna with an unusual wedding gift. He belonged to a church that practices pagan rituals centered around the visions of three elderly female prophets to commune with Jesus. Amanda's cousin asked these women to record a prophesy about Jenna and Amanda but didn't tell the seers anything about them or that the recording was a wedding gift. They saw Jenna as Annie Oakley, holding a horse that was breaking the reins. The horse, they said, was Jesus. Then they began humming a lullaby that Jenna's grandmother had sung to her as a child. About Amanda, one of the women said, "I don't know anything about Amanda, in features, but I have the sense that she is a bride. The wedding veil is over her face, in bashfulness, but she is ready to surrender. She is a beautiful bride."

# COMMUNITY

## Sarah & Julia

SARAH TOOK A FERRY TO SEATTLE from Bainbridge Island one night to go to a friend's birthday party. Partway through the night, she struck up a conversation with Julia in the kitchen. Neither of them had seen the other before. They glanced at each other throughout the evening, thrilled by each other's smiles but unable to interpret them. Sarah was disappointed when Julia went home with another girl who she appeared to be flirting with. Later, Sarah was excited to learn that the person Julia left the party with that night was just a friend who was crashing on her couch. A few weeks later, Julia found out about Sarah's crush middle school style—at a sort of single-people solidarity night on Valentine's Day, her friend said, "I know someone who likes you . . ."

The next month, Julia and Sarah ran into each other in a bar where, by coincidence, two friends were having parties. This time there was more intention in the looks they exchanged, and the friend Sarah was out with wound up taking the ferry home to Bainbridge by herself. Just two weeks after that enchanting night, Sarah was slated to move to

Orcas Island for a job. Before she left, she and Julia had a relationship-defining talk. This was a big step for Sarah, who said that at the time she was "flinging around all over the place."

A couple months after they started dating, Julia visited Camp Orkila, where Sarah worked at the time. Sarah invited Julia to try a giant rope swing, suspended from the trunks of evergreens hundreds of feet high. Julia was excited but became frightened as she got into the harness. "Don't worry," Sarah told her. "The cable holding you is strong enough to hold two school busses." Julia knew she liked Sarah a lot, but as Sarah calmly fastened her into the rope swing, she realized she trusted her as well. Years after her arboreal carnival ride, she would buy Sarah two toy school busses to celebrate their first wedding anniversary.

The idea of a long-term, serious relationship had always frightened Sarah more than plummeting out of trees. After they'd been dating about two years, Sarah realized this was the kind of relationship she wanted with Julia and fear was all that was holding her back. Upon Julia's return from a vacation in Thailand, Sarah disclosed this utterly terrifying and wonderful truth, which Julia had been waiting and hoping to hear. A few months later they moved in together to Seattle's Central District, a valley of tall creaking houses with huge backyards, and bought a few chickens.

"We have a metaphor for our relationship," Julia said. "I'm the nucleus, and Sarah is the electron. At first she was on Orcas, all over Puget Sound. We still kind of do that. I was inside this morning; she was all over the garden."

Like the parts of an atom, Sarah and Julia are distinctly different from each other but harmonious and cohesive. Sarah and Julia's cohesion is just as noticeable as their differences. They're both cheerful and outgoing, and laugh easily. They love good company, nature, and being outdoors, and have explored hundreds of miles of beaches, forests, and mountains by foot and bike. Sarah, who grew up on Bainbridge Island, has been a Girl Scout since she was a child and now works with high schoolers at the Student Conservation Association. Julia does research at Seattle Children's Hospital.

A couple years later, Julia thought it was very odd when Sarah, who is just as sociable as her, said she didn't want any friends to accompany them on their upcoming backpacking trip to the Goat Rocks Wilderness. The odd behavior continued. As they summited a beautiful peak on the trip, Sarah began gathering rocks and arranging them near the edge of a cliff. "I thought, this is weird," said Julia. "She's doing some sort of art project." Then she saw that the rocks spelled out "Marry me." "I'm so scared!" Julia said as they hugged each other. "Me too!" said Sarah. "I'm afraid of commitment!" "No," Julia replied. "I mean I'm scared of falling off the cliff!"

They made it home without falling off anything and announced their engagement to their families. Over dinner, they gave Julia's parents a card that said, "For your anniversary, we're giving you a daughter-in-law!" After a moment of confusion ("Who? From where?"), it was one of their happiest evenings together.

Sarah and Julia began to plan. They couldn't have their wedding at Sarah's old Girl Scout camp on the Hood Canal (such camps, apparently, have a no-weddings policy,) but her parents' home on Bainbridge Island was another great option. Sarah still wanted to include her camp community in the ceremony—weddings are usually largely about community, and Girl Scout camp was an important part of her life growing up. The girls she went to camp with remained close friends as adults. Sarah loves singing with other people under nearly any circumstances (her bachelorette party ended with karaoke), so naturally, she decided the ceremony should include camp songs.

Julia grew up surrounded by Jewish history and culture, passed down from her mom. Though the family was more culturally Jewish than religious, they celebrated Jewish holidays, and Julia attended Sunday school. In fact, Julia's former Sunday school and piano teacher whom Sarah describes as a "gay, secular Jewish wise woman," officiated the couple's wedding. Julia, while mostly secular herself, identifies strongly with her heritage and loved the idea of incorporating traditions that her ancestors had practiced for centuries into her wedding.

A friend, local artist Clare Johnson, made a *ketubah* (a Jewish marriage contract) for Julia and Sarah. Traditionally a ketubah includes promises made by the couple to each other and is signed by the couple, the rabbi, and two witnesses. Julia and Sarah's was made in the image of a tree. Close family members signed its leaves the night before the wedding, and the following day everyone in attendance did as well. Signing symbolized their support of the couple and involvement in their community.

Old friends serenaded Julia and Sarah with camp songs as their parents escorted them down the aisle to a *chuppah* (wedding canopy) representing the home a married couple creates together, made from Julia's grandma's tablecloth.

The ceremony began with the officiant's welcome and a blessing called a *shehecheyanu*. This was followed by the lighting of a unity candle, a tradition Sarah's parents had incorporated in their own wedding. Two small candles are lit at the beginning of the ceremony, representing the two individuals getting married, and afterward a larger central candle is lit, representing their coming together and the merging of their families. Sarah was participating in another, less visible family tradition that evening, of Welsh and Scottish origins—she wore a twopence in her shoe for luck.

Sarah and Julia adapted the Jewish wedding tradition of *Sheva Brachot* ("Seven Blessings") to better reflect Julia's relationship with Judaism and its relevance to the marriage.

Traditionally the blessings are related to God, but Sarah and Julia's blessings were titled "Adventure, Love, Growth, Laughter, Health, Family, and Community." Each of the first six blessings was made by a family member, and all guests joined in song for the seventh blessing, "Community."

The two said their vows, stepped on a glass to cheers of "mazel tov!" and then went off by themselves briefly for *yichud*, or the first moments of privacy after marriage. They giggled about this custom, alluding to some possible intended purposes for the customary time alone. "We did make out," Sarah admitted.

Both Sarah and Julia's favorite part of any wedding is the part where the guests pledge their support of the relationship, and they love basically any opportunity to sing or dance in a group. They returned to the party for some festive Jewish dancing, which started when everyone joined hands to form a sort of conga line that snaked all over the lawn. They had fun being carried aloft on two deck chairs, and watching their parents get hoisted into the air as well.

Sarah and Julia included these traditions in their wedding to create a sense of closeness with loved ones, as well as a sense, for themselves and everyone in attendance, of being part of something larger, part of history. Three months after the big wedding on Bainbridge, they had an opportunity to do something historically unprecedented in Washington State. When Referendum 74 passed, they were at the recorder's office at six in the morning on the first day gay marriage was legal. In Washington, a marriage can't be made official until three days after the marriage application is filed, presumably to keep people from marrying while drunk or in the delirium following good sex. The recorder's office is about as romantic as a dentist's office in a strip mall, but that morning, it had the atmosphere of a holiday. The recorder's office employees seemed just as excited as the couples who filed in, many of whom had been waiting to marry for decades.

Three days later, Julia and Sarah put on their wedding suit and dress and headed down to the King County Courthouse with a few family members and their good friend Emma Byfield, a professional wedding officiant. The courthouse was packed with newlyweds and soon-to-be-married couples. Outside, droves of people had come to celebrate the historic day. Sarah and Julia saw elderly brides and grooms led down the aisle by their adult children and grandchildren. Musicians gathered outside the courthouse for what was probably the largest number of simultaneous weddings they had ever played for or ever would again. It was like the Jewish dance Sarah and Julia had loved so much at their Bainbridge wedding but on a statewide scale. They walked down the steps of the courthouse hand-in-hand in a procession of other newlyweds, to a reception that filled a block and whose cheers drowned out traffic.

## PART V

# The Happily Ever After Party

# HONEYMOONS

## *Vega & Mala*

WHEN MALA WAS ONLY SEVEN, HER mother lost her hearing and grew to depend on her daughters for help. Later this inspired Mala to work in public services, starting at the Washington State Office of the Deaf and Hard of Hearing. In 1996, she moved to Bellingham, Washington, to manage one of the Office of the Attorney General's Consumer Resource Centers.

With work and housing lined up but no company for after-work drinks, Mala used a worldwide e-mail list called SAWNET (South Asian Women's Network) to look for friends who shared her cultural background in her new town. As luck would have it, Vega, who was born in Madras (now Chennai), India, and grew up in West Bend, Wisconsin, responded to her query. Vega was an academic, a non-profit leader, and a university student services professional. When she and Mala met, she was teaching at Western Washington University in Bellingham.

Vega and Mala both initially assumed that the other was straight, mainstream, and perhaps married to a man, so both were surprised and pleased to learn the other was queer. Neither had expected to find another Tamilian or South Asian queer woman in Bellingham, and they soon became fast friends.

At the time, Mala was in a long-term relationship with a woman from Western Oregon. In 1997, Mala's relationship with her partner suffered increasingly with the stress of their different cultural attitudes and perspectives. But when Mala's partner's mother was diagnosed with lung cancer and moved in with them, they put a hold on their relationship questions and issues. At one point, Mala became the sole provider for all three.

Mala's family had come to the United States from India in 1966, and her dad found work at the at the Embassy of India in Washington, DC. Mala's parents made sure she was born in Washington, DC, so that she would be an American citizen, but she spent the first few years of her life with her mother and sisters in India. She and Vega bonded over their early experiences straddling two cultures.

But they found that their similarities went far beyond heritage and sexual orientation. They both love playing and listening to music, going to concerts and lectures, having people over for home-cooked meals, and long conversations over a drink about all things philosophical, ethical, and social scientific. Both felt like loners in their Tamilian communities, as well as their broader American community.

They had so much in common, they joke that if one of them were a man, their parents would have arranged their marriage. Both have saved their early volley of e-mails.

"Our attraction to each other grew as our friendship grew, engaging in deep conversations and singing to cheesy 1970s hits and doing queer South Asian organizing together," said Mala. They became increasingly aware of their feelings for each other. Vega recalls a night they went to a concert with friends in Bellingham. Mala had just gotten a sharp-looking haircut in Seattle, and Vega couldn't stop thinking about it. After the show, they went out for drinks at Rumors Cabaret. "Mala got there first and was sitting at a table when I walked in," said Vega. "I caught a glimpse of her. She was smiling at someone and looking radiant. I could hardly breathe; she was so beautiful."

"That year challenged a lot of my thinking," said Mala. "Discussions on SAGrrls, an online queer South Asian women's forum, about how our desires, our love and attraction toward others, are so mediated by the dominant society's portrayal and definition of beauty. A debate with my cousin's husband about arranged marriages, particularly the insularity of marrying someone of the exact same race and cultural background. Caretaking for my partner's mother during the last months of her life. At some point, I wanted to be around Vega more and more. I could imagine our lives together into the future, and I knew I loved Vega, and I knew I was in love."

They'd been friends for several years before the night they consider their first date. When they finally confessed their attraction to each other, Mala was at first reluctant to act on her feelings, because of how painful the end of her last relationship had been, and because in the past she'd had difficulty building relationships with intimate partners. She cared about Vega and was unwilling to lose their friendship for a fling.

Vega suggested they have dinner and talk, so Mala cooked dinner, and then the two had an enlightening conversation about relationships and watched an '80s lesbian movie. At the end of the evening, Mala offered to rub Vega's feet. A few nights later, they kissed for the first time. "It went from attraction to head-over-heels in love in about a week," said Mala.

Over the next year, Mala moved to Seattle and then to Olympia, two and a half hours from Bellingham. Vega had been teaching at Western Washington University for five years and decided she wanted to change her career. Both wanted to live together, but questions arose about when, where, and how. They talked a lot about their differences—both valued time alone and had different standards of cleanliness.

Vega moved into Mala's apartment in Olympia, and they found they enjoy living together, though there were, and are still, occasional disputes. The two recommend couples therapy and self-help (which they've done extensively) for every couple.

Mala and Vega had always bonded over their political views and had comparable strategies for creating social change. Together, they founded Trikone-Northwest, a community-based nonprofit supporting queer South Asians, as well as a consulting business.

Mala's previous relationship, with the woman from Oregon, had been quite serious—in fact, there was a commitment ceremony involved. Two years into their relationship, Mala and Vega both knew they wanted to spend their lives together. Vega, who is a little older than Mala, was ready to get married, but because of how painfully Mala's last relationship had ended and how high her hopes for it had originally been, she was wary of another official, public commitment ceremony. "If I couldn't make it work the last time, what guarantee do I have that I can make it work this time?" she thought. Though Vega often dreamed of their wedding, she respected Mala's reticence in the wake of her last relationship. Mala knew she wanted to marry Vega but that she absolutely needed to wait until it felt right. Eventually, it did. On October 12, 1999, the third anniversary of the day they met, Mala proposed to Vega in their bedroom in Olympia.

Growing up in fairly traditional, conservative Hindu families, Mala and Vega both had great difficulty coming out, which made some of their close family members' excitement about their engagement particularly affirming. Mala's older sister, Vijaya, even volunteered to officiate. Mala and Vega each had one excited parent and one who was opposed to their marriage and did not attend their wedding but has since become supportive of their relationship. There was a mixed response from extended family. "The more progressive of our cousins supported us unconditionally. Overall, we were pleasantly surprised and overwhelmed by the support and love that our families showed us," said Vega. When they found a Hindu priest to officiate their wedding, Mala's sister became MC of the celebration.

Mala and Vega were married at the Seattle Aquarium on June 30, 2002, in an upstairs room decorated with garlands, photos, and centerpieces made by their friends. Friends also designed the invitations, helped with music, and contributed to the printed wedding program. "We felt blessed and embraced in the love of our community through the event," said Mala.

Their ceremony has become popularly known as the first Hindu lesbian wedding in the world, but Mala and Vega believe it may have just been the first in the United States. They met with the priest and his wife two weeks before the wedding and discussed wedding-related Sanskrit mantras he had looked up that referred to the union of two souls without identifying gender. Together they planned the gender-neutral, feminist, and non-casteist rites to include in the wedding. Despite the fact that Mala is an agnostic and Vega is an atheist, Mala knew long before she proposed that she wanted a culturally appropriate Hindu ceremony, as an act of defiance and reclaiming heritage. Vega mainly wanted a big party with all her loved ones. "As it turned out, we both got our wish," said Mala.

Once the guests had gathered at the aquarium, Vijaya opened the ceremonies, and the Hindu priest began a ceremonial chant. The couple took the stage, Mala holding hands with her mother and Vega with her father, and were greeted by the priest, who read the *Ganesh puja* and the *Navagraha puja* (puja means "prayer"). Vijaya performed an invocation of elders, a ritual which is used to commence a variety of auspicious occasions in Hindu tradition, and made a speech introducing Mala and Vega and the significance of various aspects of their ceremony. "The couple takes seven steps, the saptapadi ceremony, together to signify their vow to face life's challenges together, which is the central core of the Hindu marriage ceremony," she said. "There are various precedents within the Hindu tradition for same-sex partnerships and marriages: Two of the key male gods, Shiva and Vishnu, themselves were married and even produced an offspring, Ayyappan, who is one of the most venerated deities in Hinduism today. Then there is Ardhanarishvara, the merging of Shiva and the female god Parvati, as neither male nor female."

Mala and Vega fed each other milk and honey, and exchanged garlands, symbolizing the unification of their souls. This was followed by mangalyam—a ceremony quite like the ring exchange of European tradition—in which the marrying couple changes from the clothing typical of the unwed into the clothing of the married. Vega and Mala had two mangalya (ornate threads traditionally possessed only by the groom) representing their heritage, which were taken around the room to be blessed by those in attendance, before the couple placed the sacred threads around each other's necks as multicolored rice was sprinkled around them.

In celebration of their dual cultural identities and the country they had called home most of their lives, they followed the mangalyam with a Western-style exchange of rings and vows they had written. After the additional exchange of traditional Hindu vows and many blessings from the priest and all of their friends and family, Mala and Vega led the celebration into a transparent underwater dome inside of the aquarium's largest fish tank, where they danced in the glow of the tank beneath multicolored fish for the rest of the evening.

The following year, Mala and Vega honeymooned in Hawaii. "We love nature, the ocean, warmth, sun, water, mountains, abundant wildlife, birdwatching, quietude, astronomy, and observatories," said Vega. "So we went to the Big Island for a week." They saved money, planned, and prepared, and then on the way out of town, they got in a massive, horrible fight.

This, unfortunately, happened nearly every time they traveled in those days. The stress of travel set off their few, normally inconsequential differences like a match in a pool of gasoline. Mala ran late, overpacked, and forgot things—her wallet and ID, no less—on more than one occasion. Tidy, organized Vega became harsh and judgmental. The two spent the day of their flight and the first day of the trip having one of their worst fights on record. Then they remembered they were on their honeymoon, in Hawaii, and that they had dealt with conflict before and could handle it. "And then . . . it was bliss," said Mala. They even stayed an extra day. They've now traveled enough together to stop such fights before they start.

Vijaya's words at their wedding have proved entirely true: "[Marriage] is the merging and intermeshing not only of two bodies and two personalities but also of two life stories. We marry a mystery, an other, about whom we have a magnificent feeling, of loving that person in all that they are. We are each still and always becoming, and when we marry, we promise not only our own becoming but also our willingness to witness and withstand the ongoing becoming of another human being."

**NOTE:**

In 2004, Mala and Vega were one of six couples who participated as plaintiffs in the marriage equality lawsuit in Washington State. Their lives were transformed as a result, and their participation as South Asians reverberated as far as Sri Lanka and India. Though the state was unable to grant Mala and Vega marriage licenses at the trial's conclusion, the lawsuit was a milestone in the fight for marriage equality. The two were legally wed in Maryland when DOMA was overturned in 2013.

# MARRIED LIFE

## Janet & Donald

BY THE TIME DONALD AND JANET actually met, they had been in the same room together an unlikely number of times without ever speaking to or even noticing each other. They'd both attended the same concerts, parties, and even a fundraiser held when Donald, a bike mechanic and messenger, was hit by a car. They agree now that they met at exactly the right time—they were both a bit wild and reckless when they were younger. If it had happened any earlier, either of them might have ruined it.

On a visit to Seattle in 2006, Donald stayed for two weeks at a punk house called Shabang. Janet came over one night to visit friends. The sight of handsome Donald on the porch as she rolled up to the house nearly made her fall off her bike. They talked all night. The following evening, they met at Shabang again and hung out while Donald and friends gave themselves and each other stick-and-poke tattoos on the front steps. "I thought, if this doesn't scare her, nothing will," said Donald. Janet was certainly feeling something, but it wasn't fear. She asked him on a date. Janet recalled, "Netflix called the movie I brought over a gay comedy, except it was super depressing. A bunch of drag queens die." This may have been why Donald stayed rigidly still when Janet rested her head on his knee. By the end of the movie, she had resigned herself to going home alone. However, on her way out the door, Donald said, "Would you like some company?" Janet smiled. They rode her green Sting-Ray with a sparkly banana seat the few blocks to her house.

They spent every night together for the rest of Donald's trip. Donald was living in Tucson and wished he didn't have to go home so soon. By some lovely coincidence, Janet had just bought a plane ticket to Tucson to visit an aunt. Needless to say, less time was spent with the aunt than anticipated. After her departure, Donald sent Janet a little book he'd made for her, bound with bicycle spokes, that had two mixtapes inside it. This was the first of many gifts they exchanged through the mail—mixtapes, letters, clothes. Worried for Janet's safety when she traveled to Israel, Donald made her a pillow with love letters in the pockets, in place of the hugs he wished he could give her during that potentially dangerous trip. They've kept all of these presents—Janet even showed me the pillow.

During their two years of long-distance dating, they each visited the other about three times. On one of these stays, Donald, determined that Janet would have an amazing time in Tucson, rented her an art studio to work in for three months. He gathered what he hoped was everything she needed to be happy, like a bowerbird building a nest, and at the end of that time, she returned to Seattle. He built a padded box and transported all of the paintings she made to Seattle for her by Greyhound.

While distance had its charm, excitement, and top-quality mixtapes, there are parts of a relationship that can't be mailed. Donald was reluctant to move back to Seattle, having felt disillusioned with the place after he was hit by a car, but Janet's whole family lived there, and he and Janet missed each other increasingly. He came back to town, and they moved in together.

Their decision to have a wedding involved no proposal. They were at home one night recalling their adventures hitchhiking through Mexico, their visits, and all of the beautiful letters necessitated by living in different towns. They wanted to have adventures together forever. The decision to get married was the acknowledgment that their love—its strange ease, its endurance, the fact that neither of them could imagine their lives without it—was so wonderful that it deserved a party. The first step of planning, for them, was simply walking across the hall and asking a friend if he would play music at their party.

Donald and Janet's wedding began with a bike parade through the streets of Seattle to the Arboretum. The bikes were of all shapes and sizes: road bikes, choppers, Sting-Rays.

For some of those in attendance, the parade was especially exciting because they didn't exactly know how to ride bikes. Janet and Donald's friend Alex led the procession through the Arboretum to a meadow while serenading them with a viola. Their friend Ezra officiated the wedding, and the couple said exactly how they felt about each other in front of everyone they would most like to hear it.

Gay marriage wasn't legal when they had the ceremony, so Janet's marriage to Donald, a trans person who was marked as female on paper, was not recognized by the state. "I think a lot of people assumed when we had our ceremony that it was connected to the struggle for the right for gay people to marry legally. It wasn't about that at all," Janet explained. "We really wanted to celebrate our love, be with our friends and families. It didn't matter to us then that we weren't getting a marriage certificate."

The wedding was just what they'd hoped for. Both of their families were thrilled about the marriage, though Donald's family has at times been confused by him. At twenty-two, he showed his mom a picture of the woman he was dating (he had previously dated men) and she said, "Are you sure?" and then "I just hope you're happy." His being transgender was harder to grasp, as is often the case in a culture still clinging to the idea that a person's gender identity resides in their junk. Ultimately, his family accepted it with the same sweetness. His mom asked at one point whether he was going to be like Cher's daughter, and he said, "Cher who?" Before he was even out as trans, his grandma asked his mom whether he was on T. "I wondered where she learned that language," Donald said. "Oprah?"

Donald and Janet have always done what felt right for their relationship, with no regard for convention. Thus, they have a happy marriage that inspires support and affection from everyone around them, even when they are a little misunderstood.

"It's been just the same since we were married," said Janet. "Everyone's like, how's married life? Life after marriage has been just like all of life, a roller coaster of sweet and tough times. Our ceremony—publicly sharing our commitments to each other and our communities—has helped to hold things together when we find ourselves in the stickier parts of life." Donald continued to work as a bike mechanic after the wedding, Janet was still teaching art and English at a middle school, and they lived together in an apartment not far from the house where they met. The green Sting-Ray they rode on their first date has traveled with them everywhere they've gone. The only big change has been the birth of their child, Wylie.

The decision to have a child was made as naturally as the decision to get married—the two reached an age when many of their friends were having children, and they wanted a child of their own. For Donald, the desire came when he noticed that a friend's toddler recognized him and enjoyed his company so much she was sad when he left the room. "I thought, I want to have a little person looking back at me and being my little person," he recalled. They found a donor, and Janet gave birth at home. Because Donald wasn't Wylie's biological parent, he had to adopt the baby—an expensive, complicated process involving a lawyer and a social worker.

Legal marriage didn't have much value to Donald and Janet before Wylie was born. In Washington, their domestic partnership gave them benefits comparable to a married couple, but in many states this isn't the case. "It really bothers me that couple-ness is deeply connected to family security," Janet said. "Because there are lots of different kinds of families—single parents, co-parent arrangements. I don't think it's right that any family or person should be valued any less by society. They should receive as much support as a married family, queer or straight." Further issues arose for Donald and Janet after Referendum 74 passed, when they received an announcement that their domestic partnership would be transferred into a marriage. Because Donald, being trans, had changed his name, there was no record that he existed, which further complicated the process. At one point, someone asked Janet if they were married, and she admitted, with some amusement, that she didn't know, because they were still waiting to hear if their paperwork

had been processed. The paperwork finally did go though, and Janet and Donald now live the lives not unusual for young, married parents in the United States—often tired but happy, with no particular fears about their family's legal security. Janet described the "family hug" the three have every evening: "One of us holds [Wylie], and we all stand together; he reaches his arms around our heads and smiles the biggest smile ever. We all kiss and hug each other, and Wylie just laughs. Whenever I feel stressed at work or overwhelmed by all the bad things in the world, I think of our family hugs and how much I love my Donald and my Wylie, and it immediately shifts my perspective and gives me hope." Neither of them expected life after marriage to be much different, and it isn't. Donald said, "Because we got married isn't why we're together now or why we have a kid. I'm committed to Janet. We've been through a lot. We're not the same people we were when we first met. We're always changing; we're trying to be ourselves but grow."

# AFTERWORD

WRITING *BEST PARTY* PROFOUNDLY changed my outlook on love and marriage. It gave marriage new relevance in my life, but it also made me look at the institution of marriage in our society in a more critical light.

Part of this sense of relevance resulted from witnessing the vast variety of forms love can take. Sometimes people marry each other after years of platonic friendship. Others break up but get married years later. Some couples meet each other when they are teenagers, and some meet in their fifties.

There is, I think, a common misconception that most couples meet when they're young, with an earthshaking moment of first eye contact befitting a Disney movie, and then stay together forever. I was just as delighted to hear that people who stay together can adamantly dislike each other at first as I was to find out that love at first sight is not always a myth. I began to feel as if the love(s) of my life could appear at any time, under any circumstances—the variety of true loves I observed during this project completely supported Jem's comforting claim that you shouldn't look for love—that you "stumble over it."

As queer cultural history is not inherited, young people have to seek it out as they seek out the queer community, which for me has been like a second family. I've received plenty of good and useful advice about love and relationships from my straight, divorced parents, and my grandpa once said one of the most useful things anyone has ever told me about sex: "You get in bed and you roll around and it's a lot of fun, and afterward you're both just as dumb as you were before."                 .

However, to vastly oversimplify, things are just not the same for straight people, and generational differences contribute to that. The way straight relationships are traditionally conducted does influence us to an extent, but it seems to me that this model never entirely fits. Thus, each same-sex couple must figure out what works for them. There are good and bad things about this—cultural expectations of how men and women should treat each other can have harmful effects (such as unfair division of labor) that can be avoided by this reinvention of relationship dynamics.

But then, there's often a moment in which one wonders, "Am I doing this right?" I can't speak for everyone, but for me, this happens with particular frequency during the early part of a relationship where both partners are gauging how the other would like to be treated in regard to gender. One wonders, for instance, "Will she like it if I tell her she's pretty? Should I buy her this pin, or does it have too many glittery terriers on it?" Answers to these questions, of course, aren't even always gender related, which complicates things further.

Probably everyone wonders this, regardless of sexual orientation, but the less the available relationship models resemble one's own, the deeper the uncertainty. One of the best parts of this project for me was just hearing about the mechanics of relationships similar to my own and realizing that gender roles just don't really matter—the best way to establish a healthy relationship dynamic is a respectful, open dialogue between those involved.

As for what I've learned about the institution of marriage, while forty-six people are hardly enough for a comprehensive study, the interviews I conducted for *Best Party* showed me that the impression I had always had of marriage as antiquated or irrelevant is partly due to the fact that the nuclear family is no longer (if it ever was) the predominant family structure.

The couples I interviewed belonged to families of all different kinds. Carolina was raised by two women who had never been romantically involved. Kevin and Norbert raised two sons with a lesbian couple who eventually separated. While Kevin was the biological father of those children, they were essentially raised by two mothers and two fathers. Joseph and Gary had twins with a close friend who'd wanted a child for years. The three of them are now raising the babies together, though the men's romantic interest is in each other, not their children's mom. Jeffrey and Rodney adopted a teenage son who referred to a woman from a family he'd previously lived with (not his biological mother) as "mom." They were inspired to adopt by their friends' kids, whom they considered their de facto sons. Janet and Donald got to navigate conception, pregnancy, birth, and second-parent adoption as a queer and trans couple, which came with its own set of unique adventures and struggles.

This is not to imply that "family" is defined by the raising of children—Kurt and Britton would have liked kids but met when they were past the age when they felt they'd have the resources. Britton spends most weekends caring for his elderly mother. Jem and Sterling devoted their time and resources to helping AIDS patients, and thus far, Kitten and Lou's "kids" are the incredible performances they put on together. Why should people caring for each other in any configuration receive less recognition than a nuclear family? Why should the absence of blood kinship or the nature of the love between family members affect their access to resources or social services, or whether society approves of them? The glaring arbitrariness of the legal importance of the gender of the members of these families is indicative of larger problems in the way we currently think about family.

For example, I interviewed two trans couples, and I had to think about their role in the book. (An aside: I prefer the term "queer," a term that encompasses all sexual and gender minorities that are not heterosexual or cisgender, to "gay," for reasons explained below, but the term "gay" is currently more widely used. My hope is that this book may acquaint some people with the word "queer" as it is used here who were not aware of it or the reasons for its use before.) Donald and Janet are a queer cis person and queer trans person, but Donald's gender on paper subjected them to a variety of problems affecting same-sex couples, which they openly and eloquently discussed. Certainly, as two women, Alyson and Carolina qualify as gay, yet they could have married long before gay marriage was legal in Washington. Pre–Referendum 74 government regulation of marriage effectively barred a queer, opposite-sex couple from marrying while permitting a gay couple to do so—it might be funny if the lifelong mislabeling of Alyson's gender hadn't caused her extreme emotional distress and if same-sex marriage hadn't complicated Donald's birth certificate and adoption experience and cost Janet and Donald a ridiculous amount of money.

I think that most people feel reasonably comfortable with one of the two English words for gender assigned at birth based on observable physical characteristics, but I also think the division of gender into two categories is misleading, because gender is actually a continuum. Volumes have been written about this, but I'll cite my own experience. I have a fairly masculine gender presentation. I like having a woman's body, but I identify more as a man. Once, when a little kid asked if I was a boy or a girl, I pointed to a clock and said, "If girl is at noon, and boy is at six, I'm at about four." The kid looked thoughtful, and rightfully so—gender is complicated.

My own experience certainly confirms that sexuality is also a continuum—I'd say I'm about 90 percent gay. Was I still gay during the other 10 percent of my experiences, if overall I'm more gay than straight? If I'm 33 percent female, how gay are my relationships with women? I value my "straight" experiences as much as the other "gay" 90 percent; the idea of laws placing more importance on one of those relationships than another seems completely insane. Several of the happily gay-married people I interviewed for *Best Party* had had relationships with people of the opposite sex. Are they still gay? All of the research on human sexuality suggests the same answer to this question: Who gives a fuck.

My hope is that ten years from now, this book will seem dated because same-sex marriage has become ubiquitous around the world. In my fondest dreams, eventually people will have stopped feeling compelled, out of fear or ignorance, to place everything into rigid categories, and will have instead embraced the staggering complexity and diversity of human life.

The model of marriage we have now does not acknowledge that complexity. It's like a skeuomorph, an object with features that were once functional that have now become a purely ornamental part of its design, like a car with fake wood paneling. This has to do with the fact that church is not quite as separate from state as we may think. Traditionally marriage has been as much a religious bond as a legal one, and many religions explicitly prohibit homosexuality. In America everyone ostensibly has the right to their own beliefs, but Christian beliefs shaped the making of many American laws, effectively forcing those beliefs upon all American citizens.

What I would like to address in detail, however, is why writing *The Best Party of Our Lives* made me hopeful. The book is in part a celebration of *Windsor v. United States,* the trial held in 2013 in which DOMA, the Defense of Marriage Act, (the ban on federal recognition of same-sex marriages) was found to be unconstitutional. The trial was the culmination of a fight for same-sex-marriage civil rights that had been going on for over forty years. After the fall of DOMA, same-sex marriage remained illegal in some states, until June 26, 2015, when the Supreme Court ruled that state-level denial of marriage licenses based on sex is in violation of the Fourteenth Amendment. Since the ruling in that case, *Obergefell v. Hodges,* same-sex marriage has been legal nationwide, and there was rejoicing in the streets.

Certainly, there is still work to be done. It's just as ludicrous for our marital status to affect our access to legal rights or social services as it is for sexual orientation or gender expression to do so. Everyone should have access to healthcare and the ability to legally designate and protect their loved ones.

While the current model of marriage and its legal role in the United States is flawed, every time another country legalizes same-sex marriage, the dream of a world of informed, empathetic, open-minded people seems more plausible. It's indicative of a growing acceptance of human diversity, which at the very least is likely to make a conversation about overarching societal issues less difficult.

The majority of the couples I interviewed had been together over ten years and would have married much earlier if they'd been able. Scenarios like the one Jeffrey described, in which the death of a partner of ten years resulted in the loss of Jeffrey's home and belongings, and the deletion of his name from his partner's obituary (because their relationship wasn't legally recognized), were once common. As long as same-sex marriage remains legal (and unfortunately there are still people working hard to prohibit it), that will never happen to him again, nor to any of the other couples I met.

Jem and Sterling had been together fifty years when they married. As schoolteachers, they had to hide their relationship for decades. They cried in the home and garden department of a hardware store when an employee gave them heartfelt congratulations on their recent marriage. They simply couldn't believe the world had changed so much since they met that now strangers accepted and even embraced their love. Tragically, Sterling died soon after I met them, at the age of eighty-two. I was happy that his husband, Jem, had the rights of any other man in his position and that the two of them were able to experience, at least briefly, the recognition of the rare and precious thing their relationship was.

I envy couples who spend their lives together but are comfortable allowing each other the occasional adventure. I always hoped to meet someone I wanted to spend my life with—the whole "till death do us part" aspect of marriage—but for various reasons before writing this book, this seemed unlikely. Couples like Jem and Sterling provide a valuable glimpse of the dynamics of stable, lasting relationships. There were a few things that all of the couples who had been together longer than ten years said, such as that when they met each other, things got easier. Relationships require work, but they shouldn't be labor. High levels of trust and good communication were another commonality. Each couple's ways of fostering trust, communication, and mutual happiness, however, varied as much as their individual personalities.

Therein, I think, lies another common trait of lasting relationships. The couples I interviewed all seemed to have tailored their relationships to fit their own needs. This tailoring was made particularly apparent by the uniqueness of each of their weddings. I think that to varying degrees, being in same-sex relationships gave the individuals involved perspective.

After all, the traditional model of marriage mentioned earlier, the one that serves as a foundation for the nuclear family, is not designed to accommodate same-sex relationships, nor are the rituals that celebrate it. Already forced to alter the aspects of the exclusively heterosexual model of marriage that did not accommodate them, the same-sex couples naturally questioned whether it was accommodating them in other ways. "Will it really work for us to live together? Do we want kids? Do we want to be monogamous? Do we have to have a cellist at our wedding when all we listen to is Wu-Tang?"

All I'm talking about when I say "wedding" is a public celebration of love—something that exists in nearly every culture, in some capacity. And there are as many kinds of love as there are people. No one has to squeeze themselves into a model of marriage that doesn't fit, like some dusty Victorian corset. The happiness of these twenty-three couples proved that to me. That was the realization that made me hopeful about my own marriage prospects, whatever form they should take, and that I hope inspires work toward a world in which everyone has the same legal rights and access to resources, and a flexible model of marriage that embraces and accommodates us all.

# ACKNOWLEDGMENTS

THANKS TO EVERYONE who shared their stories to make this book possible, Georgia Galvin and Tom Kohn (my mom and dad), Barbara Osborne, Adam Boehmer, Amy Traut, my poetry mentor Heather McHugh, and my prose hero Jean Genet.

# PHOTO CREDITS

Page 2: © Swoon Imagery

Page 12: © Jenny Jimenez / photojj.com

Page 22: © Arthur Kuniyuki

Page 30: © Alyssa Wolfe

Page 38: © Chris Schanz

Page 46: © Lucas Mobley

Page 56: © Stuart C. Hemstreet

Pages 64 & 71: © Cleary O'Farrell

Page 84: © see Jennifer DeLeo for Nate Gowdy Photography

Page 93: © Nate Gowdy Photography

Page 94: © Yuen Lui Studio, Inc.

Pages 104 & 108: © Nate Gowdy Photography

Page 112: © Douglas Bailey

Page 132: © Lindsay Schuette

Page 152: © Lori Penney

Page 162: © Kathryn Rathke

Page 170: © Kelly O

Page 178: © Rebecca Hodges

Pages 186 & 192: © Arthur Shwab, www.arthurshwab.com

Page 196: © Jannine Young

Page 226: © Darya Husak

All other photos courtesy of the couples

# ABOUT THE
# AUTHOR

Sarah Galvin is the author of the *Stranger* newspaper's Wedding Crasher column, about attending weddings (which she was invited to, though the name would suggest otherwise). She has an MFA in poetry from the University of Washington, and her book of poems, *The Three Einsteins*, was published by Poor Claudia.